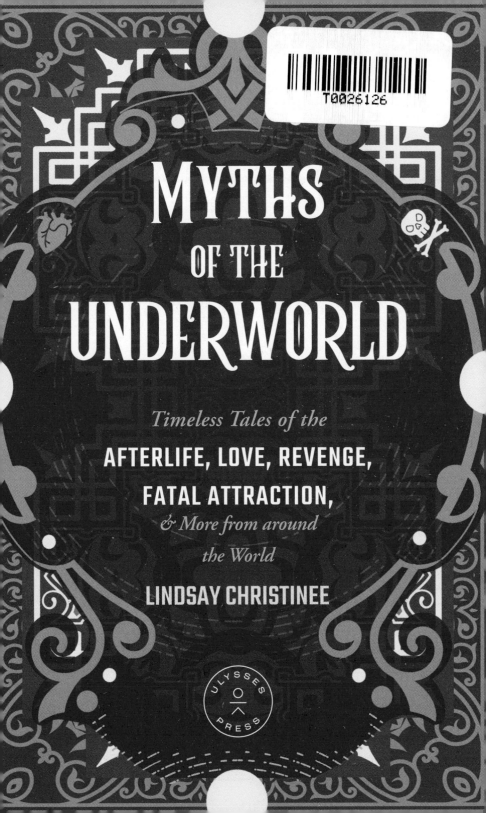

T0026126

MYTHS
OF THE
UNDERWORLD

Timeless Tales of the
AFTERLIFE, LOVE, REVENGE,
FATAL ATTRACTION,
& More from around
the World

LINDSAY CHRISTINEE

ULYSSES
PRESS

Published by:
Ulysses Press
PO Box 3440
Berkeley, CA 94703
www.ulyssespress.com

ISBN: 978-1-64604-554-9
Library of Congress Control Number: 2023938337

Printed in the United States by Versa Press
10 9 8 7 6 5 4 3 2 1

Acquisitions editor: Claire Sielaff
Managing editor: Claire Chun
Copy editor: Melissa Stein
Proofreader: Renee Rutledge
Front cover design: Akangksha Sarmah
Artwork: © Roverto/Adobe Stock

Dedicated to Emilio Drakes

CONTENTS

INTRODUCTION

I was grieving when I wrote this collection of short stories. But as I read and researched mythological beings that all had their own ties to death, it became a cathartic release that carried my pain. That became the basis for this collection of short stories: to offer the same relief to others who have experienced that same bite of loss.

One thing I've learned writing these stories is that even the very idea of losing someone isn't always as it seems. While we might view it as a loss in the West, writing this book has shown me that death is attached to many different beliefs. Some cultures and myths uphold the idea that death is simply a natural, and even integral, part of our lives. Life offers few guarantees, but if there is one, it's that we will all die. And in realizing that, death becomes charted with new meaning—one that is tied to life.

In fact, a common thread in these myths is that death is just the beginning. It's an idea that also holds true in many religions that dip into reincarnation or places dubbed heaven and hell. From the Inuits of Greenland to the Blackfeet of Montana, Indigenous cultures have long held onto their faith in spirits that continue on in a world separate from ours. Classical Egyptian and Greek myths tell of spirits and souls living beyond our bodies in realms that are governed by deities. And what's interesting is that throughout their stories, these gods and goddesses are just as perplexing in their emotions and actions as we are.

I took a lot of liberty bringing these deities (and in some cases, mere mortals) to life. For the most part, the drama is savage and emotions run high. I didn't have to embellish much there. But what I did try to draw out of these myths is a fuller idea of who these characters were. Some myths have almost completely faded from our archives, with only a few paragraphs remaining. So I filled in the blanks to craft full-bodied characters that I hope we can all relate to.

Ghouls. Evil spirits. Grim reapers. While you'll encounter some of those characters here, I don't think you'll find this collection of stories particularly terrifying. These tales are more about human connection than anything else; they are driven by desires and making mistakes.

These stories, many of them created thousands of years ago, gave life and death meaning. Some explained scientific phenomena, others simply held the essence of our joyful experience, and some even offered comfort. But in all of them, what I hope you'll appreciate is the diverse retelling of myths about the gods, spirits, and people that play an important role in each culture's ideas about death...and the life that follows.

ANUBIS

Death is only the beginning. Many historians cannot find a word that corresponds to death in ancient Egyptian texts. What they have found is the idea that our spirits continue to exist in realms similar to our own. "Judgment" was how one was believed to enter the afterlife. To be granted access to the underworld, one had to meet Anubis, the god of death. On the path to the afterlife, one would also encounter other gods and goddess-judges or those who could act favorably on your behalf.

Mummification plays a central role in one of the myths surrounding Anubis. The god was said to have been involved in the mummification of the god Osiris. This tale has been embellished to answer the question about how this process came to be and how Osiris became the god of the underworld, displacing Anubis from his deathly throne.

"We were going to change the world together. We were going to bring humanity—show them how to live in harmony with one another."

As the goddess Isis grew overwhelmed by her tears, Anubis noticed that her rich black curls were becoming matted to her cheeks. Lines of kohl streamed from her eyes and smudged into her dark skin. The crown she usually wore in those wild curls was nowhere to be seen. Even her thin dress, a slip of fine fabric that outlined her lean frame, slipped off her shoulders in disarray. But even in this state, her emerald eyes shone with a beauty Anubis had never seen before. Uncomfortable, he shifted on his golden throne.

"Please help me. I cannot heal him," she groaned.

"Why?"

Ever since he had known the goddess, she was renowned as a healer. Sometimes during the ceremonies of the dead, when he was offered sweet spices to determine whether the scent was pleasant enough for the afterlife or a curse to eternal death, Isis's name was invoked. When he'd weigh the hearts of the dead on the scales of justice against Ma'at (the truth), the goddess was called to offer assistance to the spirits in case they were found untruthful and condemned to be devoured by Ammit—the ancient jackal who consumed souls. All wise women knew to call on Isis's healing abilities before their loved ones entered death. And every once in a while, Anubis would hear mothers beseech Isis to bring their loved one back from the dead. On the one hand, she was a goddess who guarded and protected the spirits. On the other hand, she could heal even the dead if it was not their time to enter the afterlife. So why on earth did such a powerful woman need him?

"Because I don't know what to do," she explained. "For years, with the help of my sister Nephthys, I have traveled the entire earth looking for Osiris's bones that Set hacked into pieces." Her tears swallowed the rest of her story.

"I'm sorry." Seeing her frustration, Anubis leapt from his throne and knelt down by her side. "That wasn't what I meant when I asked why." He paused. As his hand rested on her shoulder, he could see how her thin dress perfectly revealed the smooth, dark skin of her breasts and belly. The fabric seemed sheer in the sunlight caressing his throne room. He drew in a deep breath. "There is no doubt that I will help you. But what I'm confused about is *why* you need my help. And what help do you need?"

Her eyes, smudged with her kohl makeup, blinked at him. Did his eyes drift from her sharp green eyes? Did she recognize the feelings that he had for her? Were his words too much of a declaration of his loyalty to her? His declaration—if it could be called that—was ill timed. Besides, what could she see in a man with the head of a black jackal?

Far outside the marble tiles of Anubis's throne room, down the columned halls and past the numerous gardens of his palace, monstrous statues were carved in his likeness. They supported the mile-high columns that everyone passed on the road to Anubis's palace. Onyx, glistening like the night, had been used to mimic his strong frame, and a nemes—a striped headdress—sat atop his jackal's snout. Solid gold represented the collared necklaces draped over his shoulders and the shent he wore around his loins. Oftentimes he wore one of leopard skin. Everything in his palace was of an unimaginable size and splendor. But it wasn't without a tinge of fierceness. When she passed by his monstrous likeness, what did she see? He took a deep breath. Of course she saw him as nothing more than the lord of the dead.

"I think, in order to help you understand how you can help me, I should continue my story about how Osiris, my husband, died," she replied.

"I'll listen." He was surprised by his own tone. It was softer than he normally allowed it to be. Regaining his composure, he mounted the steps and settled into his throne, preparing himself for Isis's story.

Isis, too, regained her composure. When she'd first entered his throne room she'd fallen at his feet onto the marble floor, sobbing profusely. Now she rose to her feet. A splash of her former splendor swept over her erect figure. She dried the tears and smudged charcoal from her face. Clearly and firmly she began her story.

"Set is sick. He only hates and kills. We all know it. The dog-headed god with an arrow-like tail. He's good only for wars. So, why did I trust a god who spews violence like a sick dog that has no master to tame his temper?

"Because, when I married Osiris, Set became my brother. And despite his reckless bloodlust, my opinion of him changed a little. I saw that he could be kind. There was a moment here and there when he cared about another living being. They were so few in between, but it still gave me hope that he could reconcile with his brother. I only wanted peace and harmony.

"It's never easy being the second-born. Osiris was the first born. His father gave him the kingdom of Earth and he inherited the sky from his mother. You know that we ruled the two kingdoms together. Have the dead told you stories of the peace and prosperity that we brought?"

Anubis could hear how her voice softened when talking about her husband.

"And for the safety of humans, we were going to spread more peace through the gift of wisdom and humanity. But Set took that from us." Her tone changed as she clenched her teeth saying his name.

"It was the first time since our reign that he decided to throw a party in our honor, celebrating our golden age of peace. 'You see,' I remember telling Osiris. 'Your brother can be kind. People can change.' I encouraged him to go to that party. I attached a pharaoh's beard to his chin to signify his distinction as a ruler amongst the gods. And I placed the atef, a feathered white crown, on his head. It contrasted beautifully against his green skin that shone like emeralds. How handsome my love looked! That was the last time I saw him alive.

"The first time someone told me that he was dead, I couldn't understand what they meant. Maybe I was in denial. Nephthys came and found me at the temple when she realized what Set had done. 'He's wronged you,' she said. I think everyone else hesitated telling me for fear of upsetting Set, the god of wrath and violence and new king of the two realms. But everyone who had been at that party eventually told me the same thing.

"There were rich platters of fowl flavored with cumin and garlic, and cakes sweetened with figs and honey. Everyone was fattened with food. Everyone was drunk from beer and sweet wine. Set made sure of it. When the music began, his banquet became a fest of drinking games. One game wasn't about drinking but about fitting yourself into a coffin. One by one they all tried to see if they could fit, but as Nephthys quickly figured out, the coffin had been designed for one being and one being only. And because of me, Osiris was willing to trust his brother. He stepped into the coffin that was his perfect fit. Set didn't waste any time nailing the coffin shut and threw it into the Nile. How drunk was everyone that they didn't realize it wasn't a game?"

Isis paused, putting her hand over her panting chest. Amongst the dead, Anubis had never seen emotion that was so nakedly clear. "I need fresh air," she cried.

Fresh air meant walking out onto his expansive terrace. The sky was red as the sun slowly set. Anubis followed, but he didn't dare stand close to her. What would he do if the hidden trapdoors of his emotions hinged open? So, he watched her—from a safe distance—as she fell to her knees. The pain in her chest only intensified. Gazing up at the sky, Isis wouldn't admit it, but all the hurt she felt was shifting inside of her. With each sharp word, Anubis had sensed the hatred swirling around her broken heart.

"Have you ever been in love, Anubis?" Almost violently, her eyes looked up and struck him. He knew the answer and would have admitted it. But something about her stare... Did she know whom his love was directed to? This worried him a little, but she didn't wait for his answer. Instead, she rose to her feet and continued her story.

"Tonight and every night since that party, Set has taken rule over Osiris's two kingdoms. And I am no longer a queen. No, each morning I have played my part as the mourning widow, dropping my tears into the Nile and taking handfuls of dirt to pour over my head. But I was doing so much more, Anubis. I was searching. I noticed every current from that night and consulted every chart of the moon to learn about the river's ebb and flow. Eventually, I found and rescued that coffin from the Nile. I pushed it onto the shores and hid Osiris in the tall grass. Thot, the wisest of us gods, was the first god that I told. He was angered by the way that Set disrupted the order of the kingship. With his help, I did something I have never done before. But I assure you, Anubis, it was absolutely necessary to bring my husband back."

Shaking, Isis continued her story. A new emotion touched her words now. It was hidden in her face as she turned her gaze away from him—shame.

"Osiris's soul had been away from his body too long for me to heal him. If only I had found him sooner. But Thot promised me that he knew of a way I could bring my husband back. We would perform a series of steps. 'First, we must prepare the body. The body cannot remain whole. We have to empty it,' Thot told me. I didn't know what he meant then. And I was too deep in mourning to question him. I was willing to do anything, Anubis." Here her stormy eyes rose and held his gaze. "Absolutely anything.

"So, I met Thot. In the shadows of a cave I brought Osiris's body to him and laid it on a slab of stone. Thot lit torches and began his work. I had never seen tools like the ones he had with him. First, he used a bronze rod to pull out Osiris's brain through his nose. I knew then and there that there was no turning back. Next, he had to liquefy and drain his skull until it was empty. When that was done he used an

Ethiopian opal to make a cut and remove all that was in his abdomen. And that's when my role came into play. I placed everything—the liver, lungs, stomach, and intestines—into four separate ceramic canopic jars. Then I rinsed my husband's body with palm wine and myrrh and cassia."

"This is why you need me? To restore your husband, after you… after you…" Anubis had never heard of this process before. But all he could feel was confusion, and immense sorrow for Osiris. Isis wasn't known to be thoughtless or erratic. No, gods and humans alike spoke of her sound wisdom. So, why then had she done the unimaginable—dismember a man and take away all that he was before he could enter the afterlife? No sound escaped his lips—but he knew what his face was saying to her.

"You must know that I love my husband, Anubis!"

At that moment, Anubis wasn't sure. Brick by brick, Isis's words were building a wall blocking his empathy and the love he had secretly harbored for years. First and foremost, he was the one who bore judgment on the dead. He was the guardian of the afterlife. No wonder he hadn't seen Osiris in the afterlife yet. But still, he didn't fully understand. Should she be judged for her abomination? He still couldn't make out why she was there.

"It worked, Anubis! It worked!"

As if Isis's words were the harbinger of light itself, the torches around them came alive, blazing with fire under the night sky.

"Tonight, I'll admit that I may have committed an unspeakable action. But I wouldn't have been able to resurrect Osiris without the wisdom of Thot. So we used necromancy, or dark magic, as you call it. But there were no malevolent intentions. We did it only out of love—me for my husband and Thot for a dear friend. When I read from *The Book of the Dead*, my words were heard. With my powers and with this process—I was able to heal my husband. I raised Osiris from the dead!"

"Osiris is alive?"

"I must continue my story."

Anubis was silent. He knew all too well about necromancy. One couldn't pretend that type of magic wasn't powerful. Oh, it was effective. But no one, especially those who used it for malevolent or vengeful purposes, ever escaped unscathed—they had to make a payment they might be unprepared to give.

Anubis and Isis walked back to Anubis's throne room, where the torches glided across golden walls and marble floors. But as the flecks of light touched Isis's emerald eyes, all he saw was revenge.

"Osiris was back, ready to reclaim his throne from his mad brother. But we couldn't make a show of ourselves just yet. He was still shaken from having his soul leave his body for so long and returning in a body that wasn't whole. Thot and I knew Osiris would need a few days to rest and restore his strength before taking on his brother, so we hid in the cave where we had performed our first ritual. For ten whole days, during which we were careful not to be seen, Osiris and I spent time together. Every night, we were husband and wife, and it was blissful. But Set had eyes and ears watching all that happened around the Nile. Shrouding their faces in black hoods and cloaks, his spies listened. They watched. And most of all, they made sure to know my whereabouts.

"They couldn't find me at first. I had my own disguises as I dove in and out of the busy markets and winding sandstone streets. But one day, I didn't notice their watchful eyes on my back. Perhaps I was distracted by the sweet figs I had purchased from a stall that day. All I remember thinking about was the joy they would bring him. Foolishly, I led them straight to Osiris.

"He did get to taste the succulent fruit. It was a beautiful last day that we had together. It wasn't until the sun set that we heard the hooves of horses thundering around our desert cave. Set had come with the full force of his army. And the way he behaved toward his brother that night was just as I had remembered him being on most days—like a dog sick with violence that has no master to tame him. Set took Osiris from me. My poor husband wasn't well enough to fight back. All he could do was scream my name. I was brought to my knees with the tip of a knife at the edge of Set's jeweled scepter pressing into my throat. And do you know what Set said to me as he drew droplets of my blood?

"'I won't make a mistake again. That coffin was too compassionate a death. This time, I will slice my brother up into tiny little pieces and scatter his bones around the four corners of the earth. That's how you'll remember that I am all powerful. But if you'd like, if you can stop this foolishness and bow to me, you can be my queen. A goddess of such power should always be a queen, and I will gladly have you by my side.'

"With one breath, Set blackened my heart with rising hatred."

"What did you say?" Anubis leaned toward the light that touched Isis's face.

Yes, she was foolish for performing a ritual of necromancy. But, Anubis could see that as Isis told the story that she was telling the truth—she had done it only as a declaration of love. Her heart still beat as the pure goddess that he knew her to be.

"I told him I would be back to take his throne—not as his queen but as his enemy."

Anubis flashed her a look of admiration. She'd lost a battle to a powerful god. But she was a ferocious goddess who wouldn't allow injustice to win the war. On the scales of Justice, she satisfied him plenty. He felt a familiar feeling rising—he wanted to help her.

"Let me guess—you need me to help you find the pieces of Osiris? Are some buried in the sands of the underworld?"

Isis shook her head.

"I told you when I first walked into your throne room that I have traveled for years with Nephthys searching for the pieces of Osiris that Set scattered. Without her help, I wouldn't have been able to find them."

Anubis knew of Nephthys. When accompanying dead kings to the underworld, he often heard her name spoken or saw her performing her role. Wailing women offered lamentations for the dead and mournfully begged her to protect them. Once, he heard tales of schoolchildren being assured not to be afraid of her—the mocha-skinned goddess with thick braids who presided over the bodies of the dead—for she was a necessary companion to the afterlife. Now, without fear of punishment from Set, she showed up to help her sister twice. While Anubis had never officially met Nephthys, he likened her to a guardian through and through.

"There is still one piece missing. If it is in the underworld, I do not know." Isis continued her story. "What I do know is that I could read from *The Book of the Dead* even without it. Without that missing piece, Osiris is alive, but not in a way that he can return to the land of the living. And that, He Who Is upon His Sacred Mountain, Lord of the Sacred Land, is where I need your help."

She was using the names priests said to him when they made sacrifices in his temples. It felt good to hear them.

Anubis settled back into his throne. Only one being could raise such feelings in him. As lord of the underworld, he weighed the hearts of humans and gods. But who was here to judge his heart, which beat rapidly at the sight of the woman standing before him? Yes, parts of her story had flicked his heart with fear, separating her with brick walls. But he was beginning to understand now. And he was hypnotized. She had used her power for love. What was more pure than that? His heart pulsed against his chest. Like Isis, he wanted to use his power for love.

"Ask me."

"If I do, please, Lord of Nine Bows, do not become angry with me." She was praising him again.

"You have my word."

"Only one piece of my husband is missing, but he will never see Earth again. Because he cannot return to the world of the living, Osiris must remain in the world of the dead. He is the god of fertility, and order would be disrupted by his presence here. A god cannot become a mortal any more than a king can become a servant. Osiris must become lord. It is the only rightful order of our realms."

Anubis avoided her gaze. Instead, he rested his eyes on the enormous torches illuminating his throne room; he traced every intricate etching and curvature of the sloping armrest. As he stared at the pools of light, he was slowly beginning to understand. It seemed that her request was far larger than he could have anticipated when she'd first walked into his throne room. Did she truly realize what she was asking?

He laughed. "Whatever it is you need, be blunt and ask me." This time, his voice was sterner with her than it had been all night.

"Anubis, Lord of the Underworld, I, Isis, am asking you to abdicate your throne."

Her honesty and simplicity was what he needed to hear. Her tears and her story—yes, in Anubis's eyes, it had all been genuine—twice had extinguished and reignited his emotions, which was confusing for the kind of god whose main role was to find Ma'at.

"Surrendering my throne could cause more chaos than even you could possibly imagine."

Isis shook her head, catching the torchlight in her wild curls. "Is that what scares you? They call on me too, Anubis. And I would never show the dead so much contempt that I would allow this realm to fall into disarray. I have already consulted the sun god, Ra, who rules over all the created worlds—the sky, earth, and the underworld—about this matter. It would be a New Kingdom, he said." She said this proudly, and for the first time in the evening, her smile greeted him.

"He Who Is upon His Mountain, you would still keep guard over the tombs from above. Lord of the Sacred Land, you would still be designated as the god of the desert. Guardian of the Scales, in the Hall of Two Truths, you would still weigh and measure the hearts of all who enter the underworld against Ma'at to determine whether or not they have lived a life worthy of this kingdom or are to be devoured by Ammit."

She was calling his names again. It was a form of praise and it was also a way of smoothly ensuring that everything in the New Kingdom would fit together. Was it soothing enough for one of the most powerful deities to abdicate his kingdom? He squinted at her, silent, allowing her to continue.

"In the Old Kingdom, you were all of these things, and you will be in the New Kingdom too. But when Osiris rises to your throne, just as he rose from the dead, he will rule, offering new hope of life after death. And that will be the difference in the New Kingdom—death will be only the beginning."

Anubis leaned toward her. She had flashed wisdom into every shadow of the transition as she fashioned this five-pointed-star plan.

"So he would offer a new sense of hope," Anubis responded.

"With a new sense of hope for the dead entering the afterlife and in the proper role as a ruler, all would be right in our realms."

"Is it that easy?"

Here Isis paused. The strength in her voice faltered a little. "No. I beg you to heal him. That is the first thing I'm asking you to do. Right now, his place is in neither world, so a new ritual needs to be performed. It is not the necromancy of Thot, but the magic I learned from Ra." Saying the name of the sun god brought back her strength.

Anubis hadn't agreed, but already there was a triumphant tone to Isis's words, as if she knew that every tear, every fierce twinkle in her eyes, every little sweep of light pressing against her thin dress had smoothly swung his emotions in the direction she had wanted, and Anubis's throne would be her reward.

"And is your next favor a way that would allow you to sit on this throne with him?"

She said nothing. A shadow darkened her features. Anubis watched as her chest rose and dropped. What emotion was she holding back?

"No," she answered flatly.

"No?"

Lightly, her naked feet walked up the marble stones of his throne. In the stillness of the room, he heard the jingling of her golden ankle bracelets. She was a few inches from him now. Her scent struck his heart, catapulting all his composure onto the cold floor. He was shaking. But Isis didn't seem to care. She took his hand and firmly placed his palm on her belly. Her skin was so warm and soft beneath the thin fabric. After a minute, Anubis understood why his hand was there. Her lean frame didn't normally have a round belly. He hadn't thought about it before, so slight was the bump. She hadn't cradled her stomach during any part of her story. But now, in the torchlight, it was clear to him that a new life was growing inside the goddess's swollen belly.

"When I healed my husband, I made love to him every night in that cave. Set cannot destroy our love. Now, I know you might be weighing my decisions. But I stand by them and by my words. I told you what I said to Set. I am not in the bloodline to inherit the throne. But as the first born of Osiris, this child will be.

"I know Set. He will try to kill our child before he is born and every day after that. And I know that a child cannot be born in the underworld. So no, I will not sit by my husband's side on this new throne. Instead, I will hide, give birth, and raise our child surrounded by the strength of the armies still loyal to me. His name, we've decided, is Horace, which means 'time.' And when Horace's time comes, when he is strong enough, he and I will be the enemy that I promised to Set. My son will reclaim his throne."

She moved Anubis's hand from her stomach. Suddenly, the air felt cold to Anubis. How quickly he yearned to feel her warm touch again. "I didn't know if I could trust you at first. But now that you have listened to my full story, what will your answer be?"

"What is that second favor that you need?"

The room was silent again. All that could be heard was the flickering of torches. The goddess looked deep in thought. At last, she spoke.

"'Imiut fetish.' 'He Who Is the Place of Embalming.' That is what Ra says they will call you. To fully heal Osiris, he says, you must embalm Osiris. Wrap his body in gauze. Preserve him so he might enter the afterlife as Lord to the New Kingdom. Afterward, all of humanity will mimic this burial practice. As reparation for your sacrifice, Ra will make this practice known far and wide so that all the priests will acknowledge and praise you for it."

Anubis's love for Isis gripped his heart. Despite her devotion to Osiris, his love wasn't faltering. Isis loved with a ferocious purity that couldn't be shaken, yet another of her impressive qualities. He had no doubt what she said was the truth. He had no doubt she would win this war. Anubis wouldn't be forgotten. He would have a new purpose and name that priests would praise him for. It wouldn't be easy—Isis was asking him to give up a part of himself for her. But he could do it, and he would do it willingly.

"What you ask, I will do." He sighed. What was more powerful than a pure love, especially when it compelled such a strong sacrifice?

"Thank you, Anubis," she said. "When my son takes his throne, I will raise him to thank you for being the first spark of hope that brought his reign of peace and humanity. And whenever this story is retold, may everyone praise you as the benevolent god of the underworld."

MICTLANTECUHTLI AND MICTECACÍHUATL

The Aztecs, whose empire spread across modern-day Mexico, believed a husband-and-wife team—Mictlantecuhtli and Mictecacíhuatl—ruled the underworld. Their names mean "Ruler of the Land of the Dead," with "Mictlan" the name given to that land. Their desire to maintain order sometimes caused clashes with the other Aztec gods.

Some of these conflicts center around creation. In Aztec lore, mankind was created four times. With each instance of destruction and recreation, tension arose between the creators and the lords of the underworld. But much like the cycle of creation, death was viewed as its own cycle. A person dies and journeys to the underworld after many trials until they are finally able to rest.

One thing I will always be grateful to the humans for—their wonder and awe.

Mictecacíhuatl's bones rattled as she unhinged her jaw. Her journey from the underworld to the land of the living would begin soon.

How many centuries has it been since the great floods destroyed mankind? How much I miss their chatter, their songs… their praises.

Her movements were slowed by a heaviness that, had she had a heart, one might have called sadness. But no, the goddess of the underworld did not have a heart. Her body did not flow with blood to beating organs like the living. She was the overseer of the dead, with a form as cold as those whom she welcomed into Mictlan, the realm of the dead. Yes, her face had flesh. Her brown skin was painted white so the elaborate swirls of black paint etched around her eyes and lips were a rich contrast. But her body, from the neck down, was a skeleton—she was a mannequin of bones outfitted in a resplendent gold headdress and breastplate framed by a flaming red cape of feathers. She looked striking. And in a few minutes, when the light of the moon completely faded, the goddess would flash like a streak of gold across the sky.

But without humans, who cares what I do? It's important to have someone acknowledge you. That's when life feels joyful. She huffed at her use of the word *life*. There was no life in her bones. There was no joy in Mictlan.

Perching on her throne, she gazed out over all that was Mictlan—the terra-cotta ground, the many teocallis (pyramid temples), the majestic mountains rising in the distance, the swirls of rivers and seas. Spray from the waves sometimes landed on rocks, but like the depths of the waters below, like the shore, nothing lived.

Mictecacíhuatl had the privilege of staring at it all, gazing from one of the largest teocallis. The other large teocallis belonged to her husband—twin temples crafted from bricks of solid gold. One could say that Mictlan was beautiful. But to the goddess overlooking a barren land, its beauty was nothing more than a shining coldness.

Mictecacíhuatl rose from the depths of the underworld. She left the terra-cotta mountains and red sky of her home. She shot toward the skies of Earth, leaving a line of glittering fire above the jaguar's heads. She flew higher than the eagles' wings, until she was in the clouds, close to the stars. But not one animal woke from its slumber or stopped its nightly routine to look up and admire the beautiful light across the sky.

Not one of these animals would care if I didn't do my work tonight. A shiver rattled her bones. The animals might not care. But gazing up at the heavens, she knew that there were other gods who would.

She perched on a cloud and began her work. Her mouth opened wide and one star fell in. She took a deep breath, and many more slipped between her teeth. With each breath she engulfed more stars until the sky was empty—free from the twinkling lights that humans had once enjoyed. Her job was finished. Now the sky was ready for the sun's journey from the underworld to the land of the humans, where it was empty of souls. With a sigh she hopped off the cloud and shot past the land of the living back to the realm of the dead.

I don't care that much.

But Mictecacíhuatl knew that wasn't true. Humans were the only ones to look up and gaze in wonder as she shot across the sky. They sang songs about her daily work. They were the only ones who cared.

Sure, Mictlan was populated with spirits who were once human. In declaration of loyalty, they bowed when they saw her. But as she emptied the stars into the now dark sky of Mictlan, so they could shine there while it was day in the land of the living, not a single head looked up to marvel. Much like the animals on Earth, not a soul here cared.

"I feel it too," her husband revealed to her.

Calendar year after calendar year, Mictlantecuhtli watched the growing listlessness in his wife's eyes. It reminded him of the soft stares of the souls that roamed the underworld—there was no purpose in their coming and going. Feelings—joy, sadness, anger—were never found on their faces. When he traveled to the realm of man, it was the same.

Only instead of empty souls, it was empty of souls. Soon, he too felt weighed down by the strange heaviness his wife suffered.

But was he not a god? Were not the strongest amongst the last tribes of humans fashioned after his impressive frame? When humans had walked the grounds of earth, they shivered with fear as he towered over them. A very fine layer of muscles bulged over his skeleton. He wore a headdress of knives and he was fierce. He wore a necklace of bones from the humans who sacrificed themselves to him. He was all powerful. So how could he feel weak now?

"The souls that descend to the afterlife leave all behind that makes them who they are," said Mictlantecuhtli.

"Why?" she asked. It wasn't a genuine question. She knew the answer, but she wanted to hear it again. It had been so long ago that perhaps now it would shed a new light on the fate of man.

"Because Quetzalcóatl, the great serpent, the god of life, believed that mankind must shed his old ways of earth in order to live among the immortals. And so before the spirits enter the afterlife, they journey for four years across the bridge and mountain ranges into the underworld until all of their memories are gone and they are but a shell of their former selves—impassive and vacant souls."

Well, that didn't shed a new light on the fate of man.

"And why did Quetzalcóatl kill off mankind?" She craved to hear something new.

"Because, when they defied him, he decided to teach them the ultimate lesson."

"He creates only to kill. One would think that Quetzalcóatl hated mankind."

"Hush! You know it is not our place as the gods of the underworld to criticize the power and wisdom of the god of the living."

Mictecacíhuatl's cheeks flushed. It had been meant as a joke, a sarcastic jab at the gods who lived above the sky of the humans. She was irritated at how her husband bowed down to those above the sky, those who destroyed mankind and left them in a state of limbo, those who had made her daily trek worthless. Silently, she turned and walked away.

Those were the last words either of them said to one another for a while.

As dusk approached the empty human world, Mictecacíhuatl unhinged her jaw to spread her mouth wide and suck up the stars she had deposited in the sky of Mictlan. Again she began her trek back to the land of man. One by one the stars left her mouth. Day in and day out, she completed her tasks, unacknowledged.

While her journey may not have been acknowledged, it was definitely seen. Had Mictecacíhuatl eyes not been weighed down, perhaps she would have looked up to notice Quetzalcóatl's amber eyes narrowing on her, observing her every move. But without her husband talking to her, without the humans praising her, with the souls being voiceless, Mictecacíhuatl was afraid to look up and realize that the maddening slowness of her life could consume her.

Mictecacíhuatl missed the other streak of gold shooting across the sky behind her flaming plumage. It was a giant serpent eying the goddess as she deposited the stars across the sky. His golden scales were ornamented with bold emerald-hued feathers that spread out into wings on either side. He slithered behind a cloud and flew down into the underworld, lurking between mountains when the goddess moped back home.

The first time the serpent saw her, he hadn't quite planned to watch her. He had wanted to talk to her. But as he peered through the clouds, he noticed that there was something off about her heavy gaze. She had shot right past him, never looking up to notice the newcomer in the sky of the humans. Every subsequent night, in the land of the living and the realm of the dead, he witnessed her empty eyes, the tinge of pain pressing her lips tightly together. Then one evening, as the skies darkened over the world of the humans, Mictecacíhuatl didn't make her trek there. She stayed in the underworld, unmoving.

The night came and went. The stars stayed fixed in the skies of Mictlan.

"This is not your purpose!" Like spears of anger, the serpent's whisper left his mouth. He wasn't close enough for Mictecacíhuatl to hear his threatening message, but he continued, "Because of this insolence and disregard for your job, I will…teach you the ultimate lesson." As these words left the serpent's lips, even he was unsure what that lesson would be.

"She's not disobeying your laws," Mictlantecuhtli said.

▲▼▲

"What's that?"

The serpent had slithered into Mictlantecuhtli's teocalli and transformed before him into a man, gilded and built like a warrior. Around his neck was a strand of beads from which dangled a single conch (a snail shell). Quetzalcóatl, the god who had once destroyed the humans, was now standing before him, ranting against his wife. Mictlantecuhtli had to defend her.

"She's not who she was before. Her mind… her will for life is gone. She's not disobeying you on purpose. She feels like she doesn't have a purpose."

It was the first time that Mictlantecuhtli had said the words out loud to himself. Each night his wife returned to their realm, her disposition was so bleak—like her mind had been trapped somewhere else—that he hadn't spoken to her. He didn't know what to say. But now, he realized that his behavior toward her had left her stranded. He knew he had to do something.

"Bring the humans back," Mictlantecuhtli said.

"What's that?" Quetzalcóatl grinned as laughter rumbled his chest. "You want me to make more humans?"

"My wife no longer has a purpose. Bring back the humans. Bring back those who praised her, who glorified her for her journeys to the sky. Bring back life that can speak, that can feel, that can pray to the gods!"

Quetzalcóatl reared back and raised his eyebrows. "I destroyed the humans."

"I know. They disobeyed you. But now I am asking that you bring them back so their absence won't destroy my wife."

Quetzalcóatl's gaze drifted past the ruler of the underworld. It was a barren land. The golden temple rose from the terra-cotta sands of this world. That was beautiful. But life did not exist here. The sun rose and set over an empty golden world. On the days when the sun shimmered across the seas, there was a lingering stillness that could make someone feel trapped inside. Mictlan was a cold world. Until now he had never traveled down to the land where the gloryless went to become former shells of themselves. The dead souls here behaved much like the cold seas that were unmoving in the distance. It filled him with discomfort.

"The humans were fun," Quetzalcóatl said joyfully. "Is that how she remembers them—shining with emotions as they called out and made sacrifices in our names? Is that why I should make humans again?"

"It would bring life back to her bones," Mictlantecuhtli said. He laughed to himself at his use of the word *life*. "Great Feathered Serpent, controller of the winds, please, for the sake of my wife, bring back the humans."

"All of us gods need mankind. All of us need to be worshiped. I didn't want to have to make more humans for a long time. But what I see in your wife's eyes is what I see in the eyes of many gods. We are all lacking a purpose. So I know that my next task must be to make humans again." Lost in thought, he fell into a long silence.

Creating humans would be no easy feat. He would need seeds, so to speak—something from which to grow the next tribe of humans. This was an intriguing problem to him. He knew what the seeds were; he would need to collect the bones from the last humans. But all of the bones were in Mictlan, and these were prized and admired by the gods. Just as humans admired gold, their bones were priceless to the immortals. It's why the gods wore the bones of those who sacrificed themselves to them. Would Mictlantecuhtli give up so many precious bones?

"I can make humans again," he said slowly. "But what I need from you, you must agree to give to me. For humans cannot be made from air. They cannot be made from water. A sacrifice is needed."

Startled, Mictlantecuhtli fixed his eyes on the teocalli, where his wife sat alone and lost. When the next sunrise came, she wouldn't be working as a dutiful god should. Instead, she would be wasting away in her own delirium, saddened by the death of mankind from centuries ago.

He put his hand over where his heart would be. *So be it. If I am to sacrifice myself for the joy of my wife, then I will.* He knelt down.

"Anything you ask is yours."

"Then I need you to show me where the bones of the last humans are in this world. For I need to borrow them to plant as seeds for the next tribe of mankind."

Right away, Mictlantecuhtli regretted his words. Certain sacrifices may not be worth the result. He was a god. He could be reincarnated.

But to give away something so prized—would his wife approve? He stared at her cold, motionless form. She was what mattered most to him.

"I stand by my word. I will lead you to the bones if that is what you need," Mictlantecuhtli said, motioning for the god to follow him as he walked down the gilded steps of his temple. It was too late to turn back. He was simply doing what he must for his wife.

In the distance, Mictecacíhuatl observed the darkness leaving the sky as the sun made its return. The faint movement of two figures caught her attention. From the corner of her eye she could tell that it was her husband descending from his temple, but the other form… Who was following him? He was shaped like a man.

But are not all the men of earth destroyed? Are they not all gone? How, then, can a man walk with my husband down the steps of his teocalli?

She barely noticed her body moving as she rose and began to follow the two figures swiftly walking through the first rays of sunlight in Mictlan. In and out of the shadows, their feet swept across the terracotta dust of Mictlan. Mictecacíhuatl stepped into the cracks left behind by their footsteps. She swung into the shadows, not wanting to be seen, squinting as she tried to make out who the newcomer was.

Neither her husband nor the figure noticed her. Far into the wilderness of Mictlan, they walked toward the range of mountains whose shores the sea slapped against. Soon the sun flashed high and hot in the sky of Mictlan. Coupled with the stars that should have been in the night skies of the land of humans, the heat struck intensely the hard waters of the sea.

Mictecacíhuatl wiped her tongue over her dry lips. She hadn't been at the base of this mountain since the last set of humans had been made. All those centuries that had passed, and now she was back at the place where their bones were kept. Her own bones felt heavier than ever before.

"When I came to meet you, I didn't know I'd be here receiving the bones of the last men from you. I didn't want to ask this of you, for I know what these mean to us gods." Quetzalcóatl took a long pause.

As god of the skies above the humans, Quetzalcóatl had a powerful position. But what was it that stopped him from telling Mictlantecuhtli the truth? He knew the bones could not be borrowed. What seeds could be? Yes, the humans would eventually die and turn back to bones. But how many years would that take? How many centuries until Mictlantecuhtli would have all of his prized bones back? Would the god of the underworld be so gracious to give them to him now if he knew the truth?

"After they were destroyed, I didn't want to make mankind again. But I know that mankind is not good. I've avoided this for as long as I could." He grew quiet.

Mictlantecuhtli led him around the base of the mountain. It was so hot that it began to make Quetzalcóatl feel ill. The air was so dry and acrid here.

"Quetzalcóatl!"

The cry startled both gods. Right away, Mictlantecuhtli knew the sound of his wife's voice. Sure enough, Mictecacíhuatl appeared around the bend of the mountain. She had heard the words of the god, and now she knew what it was that he was about to do.

"You cannot take them!"

Why do these gods of the skies always take away what we hold dear? "Four different suns. Four different reigns of man, and each time you gods killed them off!"

As Mictecacíhuatl's anger grew, her jaw came unhinged. She flicked it back into place. Snatching what was most precious to her and her husband—she spat at the thought of it. She wasn't sure why her husband had agreed. But for these two opposing gods to walk jovially together—she spat at that too.

"What do you need these bones for? Surely, not to create another tribe of mankind? What for? To have them eaten by jaguars? To have them swept into the floods? Or simply struck down in your anger?"

Quetzalcóatl couldn't pretend that this confrontation didn't throw him off guard. With each deep breath, the conch he wore around his neck rattled with dis-ease. He knew that he was too far into the underworld to seek the upper hand. Even if he turned into his serpent form, the trek back to the heavens was far. How could he defend himself against the two gods of the underworld? Quetzalcóatl abandoned any hope of saying something to appease her anger.

The god of the underworld panicked at seeing his wife. Only a second ago, she was lost in a delirious state. Now she was standing before him, seething with anger at a choice he had made only for her benefit.

How can she not see that this immense sacrifice is for her?

"There will be humans again." Softly, the words left Mictlantecuhtli's lips.

"It won't work. They will only die."

"It will work."

"No. They *will* die. And we will have to watch them die."

"Then we will welcome them to the underworld," Mictlantecuhtli assured her. "Like the sun that rises and sets in both the world of the living and the world of the dead, so too will mankind rise in the world of the living and rest in the land of the dead. By giving these bones, we will allow this cycle to continue. That is what is right."

He was closer to Mictecacíhuatl now. The heat had smeared the white paint, showing parts of the deep brown flesh of her cheeks. Even the plumes decorating her shoulders were in disarray.

"Life and death. That is the cycle of our worlds. That is what is true," Mictecacíhuatl replied wistfully. Suddenly, her tone darkened, her sharp black eyes glinted at her husband. "He will kill them all. And when the last spirit walks into our realm, what then?"

Mictlantecuhtli gave a dry cough. There was truth to his wife's words. Four times mankind was created. Four times Quetzalcóatl destroyed them all. The god of the winds was notorious for his tempestuous temper, and too often it was aimed at the tribes of man. How then could Mictlantecuhtli ensure his wife's fears didn't come to pass? He turned to look at Quetzalcóatl.

"Then he will promise that neither he nor the other gods who rule above the skies of man will destroy mankind. If he wants to safely leave here with our bones, then he must not rid the Earth of humans again for another twenty-one thousand and twelve years."

"I cannot make that promise," answered Quetzalcóatl, surprised at the god's request.

"Why?"

Perhaps it was the combined heat from the sun and the stars beating down on him, but Quetzalcóatl couldn't think. His mind felt empty. "How can I agree for the other gods?"

"Can you not ask your siblings for a favor? Can you not ask the gods to avoid killing those who worship them, those who sacrifice themselves for them? Can you not keep your word in order to gain one of the most prized possessions that us gods have?" Mictlantecuhtli was surprised at how he felt. Hours before, he had been the one submerged in fear and discouragement. But now, seeing Quetzalcóatl so direly in need of his approving "yes," he felt powerful again.

Quetzalcóatl felt like he needed to flee this heat, avoid the dark stare of Mictecacíhuatl. He had to leave this place.

"Life on Earth must continue. I will give you my word that neither I nor any god from the skies will kill mankind for twenty-one thousand and twelve years."

Favors were owed to him from the other gods. *Perhaps this will work out smoothly.* Quetzalcóatl knew that he had to be triumphant. He had to secure the bones. He couldn't return empty-handed. And he would have to convince the other gods. He wasn't a god who didn't keep his word or who stepped away from a challenge. "You have my word."

"So it will be. But if you want those bones, you must first complete a task." Mictecacíhuatl's voice was clear. "Convincing the other gods and protecting mankind won't be easy. So let this be a sign that you are dedicated to keeping your word across all of these centuries."

The white conch shell that Quetzalcóatl wore around his neck shone in the intense light from the sky. Mictecacíhuatl took two steps forward and extended her hand to lift up the shell. All gods knew of this emblem, of its sound as it summoned the wind. So small, but so powerful was this necklace that could rally the seas or destroy mankind. Mictecacíhuatl didn't feel frightened by touching such a potent tool of the other god. She barely thought or felt anything at all as she stretched out her arm.

"When I went to gather the stars before the sun made its trek back up into the sky of man, I once heard this sound," she said. "I know it well. Who could escape its mighty resonance? It was a difficult trek home through those winds. Now I want to see how powerful you truly are."

Mictecacíhuatl bent down and strummed her bony fingers across the dry sands at the base of the mountains. Here along the shores of Mictlan, one could find a variety of shells. The shell she was looking for was a conch, much like Quetzalcóatl's, only this one had no holes in it. She picked one up and brushed off the bits of sand.

"I want to see if you can summon the winds before you leave. Blow into this conch and make the sounds that you once made above. See if you can bring about the winds that blow at your command in the land of the dead."

Quetzalcóatl looked at the smooth shell. *How can I make a sound when there are no holes for the air to go in or out?* He wanted to protest, puff up into his serpent form, slash the mountains, and swallow the bones before his escape. But it would be a useless battle, one he'd surely lose along these burning shores.

How strange it is that I came here to punish this goddess for abandoning her job. But now this goddess is punishing me.

He turned the shell over and over. There was no way to conquer the challenge, but below the shell, Quetzalcóatl spotted one of the few creatures that roamed the land of the dead. It wiggled and prodded holes into the earth beneath his feet. Maybe he didn't have to concede after all? "There is a small ritual I must perform by myself before I blow into a shell. So I ask that you allow me a minute to myself beyond the next bend in this mountain."

Mictecacíhuatl glared at him. After a long period of silence, she nodded her approval. "You will have time to perform this ritual. But you must reappear and blow into the conch in front of us."

Quetzalcóatl offered a slight bow of respect before he disappeared around the bend of the mountain. He turned the white shell over in his hand as his eyes scanned the red sand for a sign of the creature he had seen a second before. The sunlight reflected over the sea. It was bright blue, like the hottest part of a fire. Not a sound was heard in the land of the dead. Not even the winds were here. How then, could he command the winds to come into a place where they hid?

But Quetzalcóatl refused to waste his trip to the land of the dead. He wasn't one to quit. At last, he noticed a small hole in the earth. Out from the dark space wiggled a worm. He knelt down to bring his face close to the ground.

So insignificant-looking is this creature that I need a favor from.

Quetzalcóatl showed the shell to the worm, pointing to where he needed holes burrowed. So small was the worm that it couldn't even offer a contemplative expression as it slid over the smooth surface of the shell. Quetzalcóatl's pity for this creature turned to gratitude as he saw the worm tear into the hard shell until it poked one hole and then two. They were fine and smooth. This was a task that all of his brute strength wouldn't have been able to complete.

How strange it is that here, in this barren land, a god has sought the help of the most insignificant of creatures?

When the task was done, he walked back to the two gods of the underworld. It had been a pleasure to greet the small worm and find that even he had a purpose that outweighed that of a powerful god. Thanks to that small creature, Quetzalcóatl knew he would be triumphant. He raised the conch to his lips. The shell felt foreign to him, since it wasn't his own. But the sound that echoed against the mountains was a familiar blast. With each breath, the god produced a strong and clear sound.

Softly at first, the wind laced around the bones of the god and goddess, playfully lifting up the feathers that decorated their frames. Then it came in stronger—slapping at the waves and pressing them apart until the smooth sea became fragmented. Between the tumultuous waves, Quetzalcóatl could see rocks. He blew harder. The waves rose higher and higher, revealing more of what lay beneath. And this time, Quetzalcóatl saw that the jagged gray edges weren't rocks but were actually bones—millions upon millions of them. He blew harder into the shell. The waves remained aloft, and there on the floor of the sea was his prize—the bones from the last tribe of mankind.

So this is why there are no winds in Mictlan? The gods keep the winds away so they may keep their precious bones, their precious secrets.

Quetzalcóatl raised a hand for the waves to stay parted like a giant wall. He turned to face the god and goddess standing in awe at the shore.

"You have seen this shell touch my lips. I blew on it in your presence. Now, I ask that you allow me to take these seeds so I might bring back mankind."

What else could happen now? Of course they had to give Quetzalcóatl the bones. He had managed to make a sound in a holeless shell. He had summoned the winds and gripped the seas before their very eyes, raising them high and gleaming in the sun.

Had Mictecacíhuatl had a heart, she would have said that she loved mankind. That she missed the sound of their whispers at night when they offered their prayers. How she vowed to bless the faithful who remembered their sacrifices to her. She would put on fresh paint for their festivities, partaking in their celebrations from her own teocalli. She longed to hear their voices again.

Quetzalcóatl didn't wait for their responses. Neither god opposed him. Neither said a word as they watched his body reshape into large golden scales. His limbs stretched and slashed at the side of the mountain. Wisps of emerald and sapphire feathers fell into the sand. Fully transformed, he launched himself at the bones of mankind, engulfing them in one swoop of his mouth before the seas came together again into a single sheet of glass. Then he flashed quickly into the sky.

Mictecacíhuatl bent down to pick up the shell that fell from the serpent's hands during his transformation. Looking at the shell, she felt confused. Why did this shell have holes? Suddenly, she kicked with all her strength and shot toward the sky. She gripped the tail of the serpent, sending some of the bones scattering around the mountains.

The deceitful serpent has lied and tricked us. This is not the shell that I gave him. He must have switched it during the ritual. The lying beast!

But it made no difference what her plans were, because just as quickly as she had grabbed the tail of the serpent, she lost her grip and fell backward with a crash. It startled her, but as she lay on her back, she felt her husband's arms around her. She knew what had happened. He had pulled her down.

"I can't believe it," she said. "When a god comes into our home and takes what we love by trickery, you, the feared god of the underworld, are willing to let him go?"

"No." His voice was firm. "We will have our revenge for his trickery. But not now. Let him complete his task. Our worlds need humans. The circle of life and death must continue. You know that too."

His grasp loosened around her. She rose to her feet. In the distance she could see the serpent gathering the fallen bones. She watched as he rose higher and higher into the sky. In several days he would be beyond the underworld, past the world of humans, and into the heavens. In several days his seeds would be planted and humans would flourish again.

This is the way that life must be. A smile lifted the corners of Mictecacíhuatl's lips. She rotated her jaw in a wide circle.

"When the moon begins its journey back to the skies of the living tonight, I will gather the stars and place them back into the skies of man."

For many nights Mictecacíhuatl made her journey. To and from the skies she went. Flowers bloomed. Jaguars stalked their prey in the tall grass. The bellies of the great oceans swam with stingrays, whales, and fish. Yes, life on earth was plentiful. And then she heard them—the sounds that had been missing for centuries.

There was a gasp.

There were whispers of wonder.

As she streaked across the sky, eyes lifted to watch her. She saw small hands thrown up toward the heavens in wonder and gratitude.

Jaguars never sang their praises to the gods for their prey. Whales never marveled at the passing and coming of each day. Only man was curious about the miracle of life, looking and wondering and offering words of joy to the gods. And they praised her as the goddess who brought the stars to them, offering her loving words in the darkness.

BALDUR'S DEATH

Perhaps you have heard of the Norse god Loki? While he has been popularized in modern culture as "the god of mischief" and is often portrayed with dark hair, Loki had a more nuanced personality and very different looks in medieval North Germanic texts. He was a trickster, and that created tension with the other gods to the point that he was somewhat of an outcast. Rather than dark and brooding, Loki was a blond and handsome giant who was a husband, a father, and a womanizer.

What's interesting in Norse (medieval Germanic) texts is that Loki was also a shapeshifter who was even able to change his sex—to be both a father and mother. This story touches on his life as a father to Hel. With a father who wasn't known to be wholly trustworthy, is it any wonder that Hel, a giant and the goddess of the underworld, often appears in ancient texts as alone and downcast?

"Hel the giantess" they called her. How many songs were there about the ruler whose face was both black and white, showing the sides of night and day? Hel, ruler of an ever-expanding realm that was named after her—Helheim. Hel, the one who gives judgment at the time of our death, spirits would call out. Did he hear her name too? Did her fame ring in her ears?

What will they sing about me on this day? For today is like no other. Today, I will welcome an honored guest—Baldur, the beloved god of Asgard.

Asgard. She twirled the word around in her mind. It was a mythical place to her. She had never seen it. But those she had spoken to said it was far from the icy winds of Helheim, beyond the world of man, past the skies, high in the cosmos. Numerous stories she'd read boasted of a crystal castle whose numerous spires jutted up to the stars. Wide-eyed, she listened to travelers who spoke of a rainbow that swept over the mountain the castle was perched on. (Later, she had to ask what a rainbow was.) Others spoke of a sapphire lake that all the gods drank from. And some, a choice few, told of cauldrons overflowing with brew beer, lascivious parties (and sometimes arguments) that lasted nights and days.

Two eyes—as dark as night—glowed back at her from the row of silver mirrors. Truthfully, that last story had been related to her only by her father, and that had been a long time ago. You have his eyes, creatures told her. But how was she to know what he looked like? What was his voice but a lost memory in her mind? Loki, the shapeshifter—did he smell like the heavy smoke of succulent meat roasting over a bonfire? Did he bask in the romantic florals and incense that some said the gods of Asgard wore? Was his head full of golden curls, or cleanly cropped wisps like the great lords of Asgard?

She sighed at the sharp contrast of her reflection—snow white on one side and black as night. Today wasn't about him. There was no need for him to be on her mind. Today, the finest silk frock in an icicle blue draped her robust frame. Her hair had been perfectly parted in the middle to eloquently show off her two sides. Layers of silver brooches and necklaces decorated her bosom. She had even opted to wear a crown, crafted of crystals twisted around spikes of silver.

She tried to lift her lips to show off her teeth. But try as she might, her muscles refused to relax into a smile.

It's better that I can't smile. I am a goddess of the underworld—she who brings judgment to the dead—not a giddy, innocent child.

A trumpet blasted in the distance. Hel felt each vibration ring throughout her fortress as the frost troll Modgud—guardian of the bridge Gjallarbru—blew into her trumpet. The golden bridge was the only road that led into Helheim.

Two days ago, Hel had spread word about her celebratory guest to all the creatures within her realm. Promptly, yards of heavy velvet, richly woven with threads of gold, decorated the stone halls. Cascades of metallic threads glistened like rows of diamonds in her fortress windows.

Hard to believe that a god from Asgard once thought to be immortal will grace the halls of Helheim. We don't have rainbows. Still, he will be impressed with the splendor of my realm.

Her thoughts were interrupted by the sound of her doors turning on their hinges. Each massive iron structure had to be pushed open by two servants to allow one of her ladies to walk through the doorway. Her long braid and robes touched the ground as she bowed deeply before Hel.

"The fires are burning brightly in the banquet hall, Your Highness," she blurted clumsily.

That's good. Helheim is a realm of eternal ice and snow. I want our honored guest to enjoy the comfort of a warm hearth.

"Is our guest at Gjallarbru?"

"No, Your Highness. But..."

How odd it is for a maiden to enter my room without having been called.

"Why are you here?"

She stayed bowed, never bringing her eyes to her mistress's watchful gaze.

"A rumor."

"A rumor?"

"No. Yes. I have word from Asgard." Her words were still clumsy. "There is a celebration in Asgard—not for your honored guest coming here, but because Baldur will not come here, Your Highness."

"Someday you'll understand that not even immortals can outrun fate. Leave. And I want you to be thankful that my temper is dull today," Hel sighed to her lady, turning away.

These should have been the last words Hel needed to say to her. She should have quietly left the room. Instead, Hel felt a strange urge to turn around and look more closely at her. There was something familiar about the piercing black eyes. They looked oddly wise and out of place against her youthful features.

"Don't you want to know what Frigg says about you? Don't you want to know why the queen of Asgard encourages the other gods to drink ale and brewed mead, because the goddess Hel will never…"

Hel's mind shot back to a time when someone else had recounted rumors to her about the gods of Asgard drinking merrily. The memory flashed like a blade. Her heart felt ripped open, and she suddenly feared the person who stood before her. She wasn't a clumsy maiden with a golden braid. Those eyes that stared back at her could only ever be Loki's. She remembered that much about him.

"Fath…" she stammered. The word wouldn't form on her lips. After all, how could she call someone she barely knew *Father?* "Show your true form to me."

She wanted to scream at him. *Out of all the days, months, centuries, why today? Why must you come today?*

Her first memory of her father: when she was a child, he had appeared to her as an old lady named Pokk. She'd said that half of Hel's face was as somber as the night, while the other side was sickly white and cold-looking—so hurtful to hear. Years later, he made a brief appearance, expressing a desire to drink with "a great ruler." He gifted her with mead from Asgard and recounted how just the other night he had shared the same drink with the goddess Iounn, known for her youthful beauty, who lifted her skirts for him. Hel knew then and there that she didn't like him. But Loki was a master of words just as he was at shapeshifting. At first they were offensive, but they could smoothly switch to soft compliments. *Men will bow before your fierce appearance, my beautiful daughter*, he had once told her. *No hall in Asgard is as grand as that in Helheim*, he had drunkenly cooed.

Now, he was transforming before her from a soft-spoken maiden with a slight frame to the handsome giant with golden curls and devilish black eyes that some said destroyed with just a wink. Back in his normal form, he gazed lovingly at his daughter. It was nakedly clear that he had more to say to her. But whatever tale he had, whatever story from Asgard he felt obliged to share with her, Hel wasn't interested in hearing.

"Good. Now, I see your face. And now you can leave."

Hel didn't wait for more words to come out of his mouth. She hurried from her private chambers down the long, winding halls. Moving in step with her dashes around corners, Loki followed her closely. Finally, she stopped outside the throne room's solid gold doors, each spanning a mile.

Some great kings and queens had guards standing outside where their ruler sat upon a throne. She had done that twice, with two separate sets of guards. Now, she knew that the greatest protection she had against enemies was the truth.

The only being standing guard outside of her throne room was Volva. Some believed she was an angel, a statuesque being of light who neither ate nor slept. Others simply referred to her as a seer. But all feared her for knowing all things and speaking solely the truth.

"Ah, good. Let the seer recount the words that your father has already told you," Loki jested.

"I wouldn't be a great ruler if I trusted only a rumor."

"Rumor? Never! I've come only to bring a warning and to help my daughter with what I saw with my own eyes. Frigg—the goddess of fertility, a seer in her own right, and Baldur's mother—has found a way to save her son from death."

Hel pretended she didn't hear him. Ever since she could remember, her father's words had landed on her heart like rocks. Today was too important to be unnecessarily distracted by emotions. She kept her gaze on Volva, who was awakening to the presence of the two beings standing in front of her.

Volva's eyes flickered open.

"I know why thou art here, Hel, ruler of Helheim, daughter of Loki," Volva's voice echoed like a chorus of whispers. "Here for Baldur, the mead is brewed. The shining drink, and a shield lies o'er it. But their hope is gone from the mighty gods."[1]

Hel smiled triumphantly. During the last full moon, she had first heard the seer speak about Baldur's death. She had been doubtful then. The gods of Asgard don't die. Yes, immortals can be killed, but doing so is unheard of. So for three nights she woke up in a sweat and made her way down to the throne room. She asked Volva about Baldur. She questioned his death. Each night, the answer was the same. Baldur would die. On the next full moon, he would arrive at Helheim. Eventually, Hel was satisfied with the knowledge that she would welcome the god to the underworld. She had sent word that reached as far as the ice trolls at the border of Helheim. *Offer the finest mead and celebrations to Baldur. Blow trumpets. Glorious is this occasion.*

---

1   Henry Adams Bellows, The Poetic Edda (New York: The American-Scandinavian Foundation, 1923).

"Steal the life from Odin's son. I saw for Baldur, the bleeding god. The son of Othin, his destiny set. Famous and fair in the lofty fields. Full grown in strength the mistletoe stood,"[2] the seer continued. Suddenly, her tone shifted. Her words began to quickly stumble over one another. "No one of men shall seek me more till Loki wanders loose from his bonds, and to the last strife the destroyers come."[3] She fell into silence and stillness, an unmoving statue again.

"I never did learn how to properly interpret Volva's words," Loki leaned in to whisper.

His smile made her feel ill at ease. *How can my father jest when we are speaking about his own death? And my seer refuses to speak more?*

"There is nothing to interpret. Baldur will die. And you…" Her voice trailed off into silence. Her father had never expressed love to her. And as far back as she could remember, neither her to him. But hearing about him in bonds felt heavy on her heart. She didn't leap at repeating the words, even if he would "wander loose."

She turned as the heavy gold doors of her throne room opened. The ceiling—a crystal dome reflecting light from the ice mountains outside the castle—swept high above their heads. Sharp light from the immense windows danced around the expansive room. Mirroring the shape of the mountains sat her throne. It was the largest quartz of Helheim. The ice trolls had sliced their axes into it to craft a rough outline of a seat for Hel. As her fingers swept over the cloudy stone, she couldn't help but feel a tinge of delight in its splendor. Was her father also impressed with all that was hers?

Loki's long fingers slowly slid over the hard surface of her chair, and he returned to his provocation. "The gods are drinking mead from crystal goblets at this very moment." He paused dramatically. "In fact,

2   Bellows, *The Poetic Edda.*
3   Bellows, *The Poetic Edda.*

before I came to visit my daughter, I was in Asgard lifting my cup in a toast to Frigg. Do you want to know what we were toasting to?"

The truth never came out easily from Loki. With his stories, he preferred to waltz. Words turned and playful banter spun around until finally the full story was revealed.

"The creatures of my court will be here soon. Speak quickly or leave."

"The glasses are quartz," Loki said, his fingers lightly skipping across the throne. "Reminds me of this stone. It glimmers and catches the light, but you can never fully see what's inside. It's clouded like a mystery. So when Frigg and I raised our glass to toast, I wasn't entirely sure what she had poured inside."

He paused, seemingly lost in thought as he smiled to himself. "I mean, death did cross my mind as I drank. The gods didn't exactly invite me to their soiree. And she wasn't entirely pleased at my arrival, despite being a very diplomatic hostess. No, it was a party for everyone else in Asgard. 'Bring your fiercest weapons,' Frigg had told them. But why not invite Loki when every god in Asgard was asked to bring his weapon, or his fists if he so chose? Does the great god Loki not have weapons? Anyway, do you know what she demanded they do with these weapons?"

Here was another dramatic pause. He stood in the center of her throne room now, looking up at his daughter. "Frigg demanded that every god strike Baldur. Yes, my dear, in drunken revelry, every weapon known to god and man and the underworld—from shield to rock to sword—was thrown at Baldur. But how could this be? How could Frigg ask anyone to hurt her treasured son?"

Hel consciously steadied her breathing. Did he notice her nails digging into the quartz of her throne? Did he see how his words rattled her? *What madness is this? How could Frigg, the goddess of fertility, foolishly behave this way to bring about her son's death?*

"'Why, Frigg,' I asked, 'What is this? How can you stand so calmly (with a drink in her hand, no less) and ask the gods to hurl weapons at your son?' At this the goddess laughed. 'Look,' she told me. And look, I did. There was Baldur, the shining son of Frigg and Odin. You'd really like him. He truly is a beautiful specimen. He has an aura about him that reminds one of birds singing, or sunshine, maybe. Anyway, he stood in the center of the great marble hall. Freyr stood to the side, his elfin blade in hand. And with the strength of ten boars he charged at Baldur and struck. And do you know what I saw? The blade bounced. It skipped across his skin, and the pretty god smiled without a scratch. I saw this happen again and again with every spear, rock of great size, and sword that was aimed at his flesh.

"'What magic is this?' I asked my dear Frigg. The goddess told me that it was no magic, but an oath. When news had spread of Baldur's death, she traveled all the known worlds and asked every living or inanimate thing to swear an oath not to hurt her son. 'Every living or inanimate thing?' I asked her. Frigg winked at me and pulled me close to whisper in my ear that she did not ask the mistletoe, for it was such an 'inconsequential thing.'

"Well, I was so impressed by her genius plan to save her son. 'I do love a bold woman who can laugh at the hands of fate,' I said to her. 'Let us toast.' This must have made the goddess smile, for she quickly offered me a drink. 'To Baldur,' she said.

"But my toast wasn't to Baldur's good health. Like you, my dear child, I believe that even we gods must one day accept our fate." The playful manner that had dominated most of his tale was gone now. A somber shadow seemed to sweep over him. He had pranced all about the room. But now he stood close to her throne. Dropping to one knee, he deeply bowed before Hel. From some hidden pocket in his cloak, he pulled out a large twig with small round berries decorating its branches. "I give you, my daughter, the only thing throughout all known realms that can kill Baldur. My toast with Frigg wasn't to life. I made a toast to Baldur's death!"

"And what am I to do with it?"

Hel didn't lean forward to touch the branch. She had wanted to. As the goddess of a realm eternally in ice and snow, she had never seen a living tree branch like this one before. But every bone in her body felt like it couldn't move.

"The feast is still going on as we speak. Let me shift into a great Kori bird and fly us together to Asgard. And then my daughter, I want you to hurl it. With all your strength, launch this branch at Baldur's chest," Loki implored.

Her whole life as the ruler of Helheim, she had welcomed many beings into her realm. There were warriors who came to her with the rally of a battle cry still on their lips. Men who had spent their entire lives in disbelief of the gods and the world beyond earth, but who bowed and sang praises when the giantess stood before them. They all had their own stories to tell. But she had never met anyone who could use words the way Loki did. Within the span of a few minutes he had managed to tempt her to do something she had never done in all her years alive.

"Leave Helheim?" She could barely whisper the words. "I can't. Leave my kingdom just like that? And to whom? For how long? Nothing you say, Loki, is ever the full truth."

And there it was. She had said his name. He was Loki. She had heard his name spoken of more than she had heard him speak. And it wasn't "Father." Loki the shapeshifter. Loki, bringer of chaos. Loki, who took a false oath with a goddess to learn how to kill her son. He was a man whose name rang with a certain kind of fame.

"No. I will not leave."

"But my child—" Loki pleaded.

"I am not a child! I am a queen!" She rose from her seat, her full frame towering over him. "Do you see this throne, carved from the finest quartz? Look at this room! There are entire cities of man that can't compete with its splendor. And do you know who I am? For centuries I have been the goddess welcoming mortals to eternity. All living creatures must come through me. And the living do not dare to disturb my realm until it is their time. I am the keeper of the dead. And I know who you are, Loki. They call you the trickster, the shapeshifter, the woe of the gods. There is a reason that every god of Asgard was summoned except for you. Just as Frigg should have done, I will not listen to your words anymore. I will not toast to you, Loki. And I will not fly off with you. I am Hel! I am a queen. I know my place, and it is not with you."

This was everything she had wanted to say to him for a long time. It all came out in one long breath. Was she wrong to feel satisfied that his eyes began watering? There was something else mingled with that feeling, too. After a brief hesitation, she realized that what she felt was regret. All her life, she had wanted her father more than anything. He wasn't perfect, by any stretch of the imagination, but today he was here. Yet, somehow, after her words she felt like a door was closing. And there was a tinge of fear that it might not open again.

"Please leave." But she didn't want to address any of these emotions anymore.

"As you wish, Your Highness." Dejected, Loki turned on his heel and slowly walked out of the room. The gold doors closed behind him.

▲▼▲

Loki tilted his head back to stare up at the hall's ceiling, so high it may as well have been the sky. He looked up until he felt his eyes drying. He wasn't one to cry. He wasn't one to beg, either. He had toiled to make amends. Yet this was something his daughter simply didn't desire. What more could he do?

For a moment he twisted this question around in his mind. He had prostrated himself before his daughter. "I'm a queen," she had haughtily told him. He had offered her the one thing that could slay Baldur. A part of him had taken pleasure in the thought of them doing something together again. It had been a long time since that night they shared strong mead and drunken stories of his life at Asgard. He knew how enamored she was with Asgard. *This memory feels like birds singing, like sunshine. He laughed to himself.*

Loki exited Hel's castle. He clenched the mistletoe between his teeth and stretched himself out into a Kori bird. With his expansive wings he flapped into the icy air, rising higher and higher until the castle was a white dot behind him.

It might not be with my daughter. But I can still do something for my daughter.

Volva's words rang too loud in his mind for him to hurl the branch himself. He knew that no disguise would stop Frigg from finding him if she learned he had betrayed her secret and killed her son. And being bonded was not something he wanted in his future. It would take only one god to throw the mistletoe that would strike down Baldur. And Loki knew just who.

Frigg, the goddess of fertility, wasn't without her flaws. Perhaps her biggest one was that her love did not equally spread to all creatures. Just as she had overlooked the mistletoe, calling it weak, so too did she overlook her son—her other son, that is. As beautiful and perfect as Baldur was, Hoder was imperfect to her because he was blind. But he wasn't deaf. While he may not have been able to see the disdain on his mother's face, he heard it in her words. How often had Hoder heard her praise Baldur's beauty? Who could recount all the times that someone said, "with Baldur's great strength he did so and so" or "how his kindness helped so and so." *Baldur* meant *great one*. *Ho der* meant *blind god*. This was all his mother could think of when she gave birth to a blind god.

Loki knew Frigg. He knew that although she was a mother, meant to extend her love to her children, she was a woman who most of all loved beautiful things. So, while Baldur was the apple of her eye, she often forgot to extend her words of love and praise to her other son. During all the parties that he had attended in Asgard, Loki rarely saw Hoder. Frigg's blind son was often kept away from festivities. Just as he predicted, tonight he'd been kept far from the main halls of Asgard, relegated to a small tower.

The blind god was sitting by a window. It was clear that he was frailer and weaker than his beloved brother. And his garments weren't of the same fine golden silk threads. His wavy red hair fell over his shoulders in disarray. Even his beard was in need of a good grooming. But the god looked content placing a magic shell to his ear so he could listen in on the festivities. Much like his brother's, there was something sunny about his disposition.

"Are they having fun?" Loki asked the god as he entered the tower. "Your mother is a clever woman, creating a joyful game to mock fate."

"It's okay. Nothing has hurt Baldur, so that is good."

"Why of course. Who could refuse Frigg's request not to harm the beloved Baldur?" Loki cooed. "Do you wish that you were there too?"

"It's okay. I don't really enjoy parties. The music I like. But other than my brother, few of the other gods reach out to talk to me."

"Ah, yes, talking at such a rowdy event can be nerve-racking. It's best to enjoy it from afar. So how will you partake in this celebration?"

"Oh. I'm happy to sit here and listen to their laughter and fun games."

"Nonsense. You deserve your fun too." Loki's eyes spanned the sparse room as though he were looking for something. "Let's see. All the gods are taking their aim at Baldur. Let's see. What can you throw?"

"Loki," said Hoder, turning from the window. "I know your voice, and you know I cannot see. I cannot aim and throw."

"Hoder, brother, beloved son of Frigg. Let us partake of this game together. And know it would be my honor to guide you. Let me be your eyes and brother for tonight, so we both might enjoy the fun." Loki reached into his pocket and pulled out the mistletoe that just an hour before he had offered to his daughter. Gently, he placed the branch into Hoder's hands, guiding his fingers over the wood and berries.

"An innocent branch with red berries. So enamored was I by this plant that I plucked one branch for my daughter. I will let you have it. It's an insignificant thing, as you can feel. But it might be fun to hurl it at your brother. I wonder what he'll say when he realizes he's been hit by berries!" Loki burst into a jovial laugh as he led Hoder to face the window.

It was working out beautifully. Hoder was standing by the window, mistletoe in hand. Loki pointed his shoulders down a bit and tilted them more eastward. Smiles spread across both of their faces. Hoder listened to Loki's instructions well. With a graceful swoop, he stretched his arm back and launched his weight forward, letting the mistletoe leave his fingertips. Eastward it flew. Loki realized that the god was much stronger than he looked. Neither god heard the branch crash through the crystal windows of the great halls, where it continued on its journey until it landed on Baldur's chest. Neither god saw the color drain from Baldur's sunny cheeks or watched as his muscles gave a final shake as he fell limp and unbreathing on the hard tiles.

They didn't see. But they heard. Frigg was the first to scream. Her screeching cry made Hoder jump back as he put the shell to his ears.

"She won't stop crying!" Hoder yelled at Loki. "What did we do? What did I do?"

Loki placed the shell to his ear. The flutes and harps that filled the halls with revelry just a second earlier had all stopped. He could hear the screams that bounced around the walls.

It is done.

Hoder, too, screamed in pain as the realization sunk in. The god fell to his knees, pounding his fists in frustration against the hard floor.

"I am sorry, my friend. I don't entirely know what happened." Loki didn't bend down to try to console him. His words landed flatly. "Perhaps it was a weapon of a magic metal that struck his chest. I will go and see what happened." Loki turned to leave the room. Suddenly, a thought came to him. "Take comfort that it is meant to be. Not even we gods can outrun our fate."

Amid the pain that Loki had caused, he could only see it as necessary. This was how things were supposed to be. Panic quickly struck him as Volva's words rang in his ears again. But quickly he caught himself. If his fate was written, so be it. And with Hoder still crying at the death of his brother, Loki quietly left the room.

▲▼▲

Hel felt the vibration of the trumpet. But instead of a single blast, it was two directly following one another. Then there was a pause, followed by the double blasts again. Modgud was letting her know that Baldur had come.

The goddess sank back into her throne. Her father had been wrong. It wasn't as he had predicted; Frigg hadn't found a way to outrun fate. What could the goddess have been thinking anyway if she was hurling weapons at her son for drunken fun?

Hel scanned the men, women, creatures, and gods in her throne room. Candlelight erratically flickered and cast a warm glow across their faces. The white light of day was gone. Outside her castle hung only darkness; within were candles and roaring fires. Hel nodded with satisfaction that it was beautiful. She was ready to welcome the first god of Asgard into Helheim.

When the god walked through the threshold and into her throne room, at first she felt sorry for him. The hidden part of her role as ruler of the underworld was feelings of pity for those who passed through her realm. Everyone had a look like they had left others behind. It made her stomach hurt and chest tighten, since there was nothing she could do except console them that perhaps in a few years or centuries they might see their loved ones again. But as Baldur neared her throne, however small he was, her pity faded. For after seeing his face up close, unlike the others, there wasn't the same feeling of loss. Instead, his smooth brow showed only acceptance, as if he were merely going for a walk on a cold spring day.

"Your Highness. It is my pleasure to meet you," Baldur gracefully bowed before her. Her father had been right that the god was beautiful to look at. His skin and hair were both the color of gold, and even his rich amber eyes were flecked with gold.

"Baldur, god of Asgard, son of Frigg and Odin. Do you know how you died?"

It was customary for the dead to be asked this question upon their arrival to the underworld. Better to ensure they understood they were dead and could accept their fate than to have the heavy truth come to them later. Those situations never ended well.

"A mistletoe." The god smiled. He seemed to find it amusing. "Do you know that it's not even a real plant? It can grow only on another tree or shrub. But when it does, it's beautiful. It flowers and has red berries. I didn't eat those berries, if that's what you're thinking. I was only struck in the chest with it."

"Who struck you?" Hel gasped, leaning forward. There was that tightening in her chest again. Only this time it wasn't pity. The banging feeling in her body felt like fear that she had been wrong.

"It was a game the gods were playing. My mother made every object in all the known realms vow that they wouldn't hurt me. But she forgot one. She didn't ask the mistletoe. And when my brother wanted to play, he thought it was so innocent that he threw it at me."

Hel regained her composure. Baldur might have not known it, but he was verifying that every word spoken by her father had been true. *It wasn't just a story.* He was also confirming where her father had gone after their meeting.

"Do you hate him?"

"Not at all." Baldur looked taken aback by her question. "He may not win the admiration of the other gods of Asgard. But he wins mine. My brother is the kindest friend I have. We are brothers. He loves me. And I him. And I know with all my heart that it was a mistake. Even if it wasn't, if for some reason my brother harbored malice against me and threw that plant to have me meet my downfall, I'd forgive him and still love him. But I don't think that's the case."

My father was right. I do like him. He isn't just a beautiful face. He's a beautiful soul. And he's one that surprises me. When all stories blend together, it's nice to feel surprised sometimes.

"Baldur, son of Frigg, and the first god of Asgard, welcome to Helheim. Welcome to the afterlife."

PERSEPHONE

The ancient Greeks also believed in life after death. For them, the soul and body were separate and after death, the soul went on its own journey to the underworld.

From a maiden of spring to the goddess of the underworld, Persephone is perhaps one of the most popularized rulers of the dead in Western culture. In Greek mythology, the queen's tale begins with an abduction and marriage to Hades, the god of the underworld. But throughout her reign, her story blossoms as her strength grows, and she becomes a fierce ruler in her own right. Perhaps, during a time when women had few political rights and were controlled by men, Persephone's story was a declaration of independence from the patriarchy that women could both relate to and emulate.

"I will always be thankful for your love, because it has always been you, Persephone, who was meant to be my queen. It's you who saved me from my entrapment of loneliness."

"Why do you think I would ever love you?" They were words meant to cut, not a real question. Persephone didn't respect Hades enough to acknowledge his love for her, if it could be called that.

Few torches were lit in the castle's hallways. But even in the dim light, she noticed thick tufts of green and black mold spurred on by the endless dampness sweeping in from the lake surrounding the castle. Every day since she had arrived to be his wife, Persephone watched spindles of green mold inch into larger clusters. It was the only thing that grew here. She was so afraid of touching it, she made sure that her feet were always clothed in sturdy sandals, and she would have rather cut off her hand than let it touch one of the stone walls. The mold, like the constant darkness and everything here, made her sick with disgust.

Looking into the eyes of the King of the Underworld spurred a sickness caving her stomach. His scheme for acquiring a wife had taken away everything she held dear. How could she love a man like that?

"Because, once you lean in and accept me, I will give you everything—all that your heart desires, my beautiful Persephone." Hades's bright, confident smile contrasted his dark beard. It swam up the sides of his face into a soft wave of curls that Persephone had torn from the first night they had been together. But his black eyes hadn't reacted. In fact, she had gotten a sense that he had kind of liked it, the way he seemed to now as he leaned in toward her.

"You are a queen of a never-ending realm. All will both fear and love you. But no one's love will ever match what I feel for you."

"I don't care about being queen. I hate the very idea of ruling."

Hades laughed. Persephone's eyes narrowed at his insolent, carefree attitude. He had kidnapped her for no other reason than to make her his wife in a false ceremony in the underworld. He made false declaration after false declaration of his love for her. She turned away from the boyish grin that spread across his sharp features. Far beyond the moldy walls of this castle, past the Hound who stood guard, beyond the lake and the rivers, past the hollows of the earth, was a place she had once called home.

"I promise to love you. And as you are my companion, so will I become yours. You'll never feel lonely here, Persephone." That grin—which had an ounce of cheekiness—was gone. Hades held her stare. There was a pleading tearfulness to his eyes. Was he sincere?

"Why won't you let me go if you love me so much?" This time, the question was genuine.

"Because a king should never rule alone."

"This castle is cold, dark, and disgusting, just like you, Hades. I hate it here—always have, and always will."

"Someday, Persephone, someday soon, I know you'll call these halls home. I hope you can call me your love then too."

How could someone be so arrogantly contemptuous?

Persephone lay awake, staring into the darkness. It was the only thing to look at in a place like this—the blades of darkness twisting and slicing her open little by little until all manner of light was cut from her soul. *There used to be light inside of me. I wasn't always filled with melancholy rage.* Persephone sank into the cushions of her massive, cold bed. Before this place, she would lay her body in fields of helianthus—vibrantly yellow and fragrant, velvety flowers—whose brightness almost outshone the sun, Helios. Persephone would drink in Helios's warm, delectable, life-giving light. *When Hades noticed me lounging in those fields of gold, did he "love" me then? Did he really think this cold bed of darkness could compare with the warmth of Helios?*

"Throughout all the Earth and known realms, I have never seen anything as beautiful as you."

The first time she met Hades, he hadn't even bothered to be polite and introduce himself to her. No, he had the audacity to make those obnoxious declarations of love. At the time, she had ignored him. Beautiful goddesses like herself were used to having compliments come their way. *Your hair shines like ripples of light from the sun,* men would say to her, or they'd tell her that they had never seen eyes as vibrantly green as hers. Worst of all was how her curves would evoke lust-filled words of praise. Naked lust was never an attractive trait to her.

Persephone repelled all her suitors like gnats that swarmed and threatened your perfect summer's day. But she should have known that Hades was different. He was more repellent than all the rest—he was a mosquito that bit and bit until it sucked all the blood from her. His swarm of black horses cut through that field of beautiful sunflowers. Was the golden chariot they pulled meant to impress her? Were his words?

"I promise to love you until the end of all time and make you a queen among queens, Persephone. They will sing praises about your beauty and your throne for centuries."

Did he even care how she felt? No, he must not have. He hadn't even given her time to make a sound in reply. Before she could leap away, Hades, with deft skill and power from his golden chariot, turned the world against her. Her beloved field of golden flowers caved beneath her feet, and the depths of the earth swallowed her whole before spitting her out into the underworld.

"You are home, my love." His cold words vibrated like a stabbing pain in her heart.

"But I'm the goddess of spring… not the underworld," she replied. She hadn't been able to form the words she wanted to. Words couldn't describe her pain. Only her tears could. So they spoke for her—night after night, her tears flowed until finally, she cried herself to sleep and there was silence.

Tonight, though, might be different. Perhaps tomorrow, I will finally be able to return to those golden fields.

On the day she was kidnapped, Helios had noticed that Persephone's smile was gone from under his warm light. Instead of enjoying her thankful smiles, he observed a strange thing—the earth had swallowed her up. *There were four black horses pulling a golden chariot.* He relayed what he saw to Demeter. It had been hard to look into the eyes of the clearly grieving mother, who brought fertility to the earth, and tell her that he just saw her most beloved and cherished child sink into the earth.

Demeter began roaming the known corners of the earth for her daughter. All the gods knew that. All of mankind, too, because they were hungry and cried out to Zeus, the king amongst the gods, that Demeter's crops and grains were dying. They begged for someone else to take on Demeter's quest for her daughter so she could return and make the earth fertile. So Zeus did what any faithful god, father, and husband would do. He set out to negotiate with Hades. And he would arrive soon.

Slowly, Persephone's tears eased as she sank into her pillows. *Tomorrow, in the depths of the underworld, my father will come to take me home, to rescue me from the hands of Hades.*

No sun, moon, or stars lit up the sky of Hades's realm. ""It [the narcissus] was a wondrous thing in its splendor. To look at it gives a sense of holy awe to the immortal gods as well as mortal humans."[4] These were the words Hades had said to Penelope when she inquired about the infernal blackness of his realm. Her stomach churned. How was it that the lord of the underworld twisted every word into an ode of love? *Hades is too cold to love.*

As she stared into the dark, a sliver of light swept over her face. This struck her as odd—where would a light come from in a black sky?

"It's Earth," Hades said to her during breakfast.

---

4   Homer, "Homeric Hymn to Demeter," trans. Gregory Nagy, 2000.

Since her arrival, he had insisted that they have breakfast together every morning as husband and wife. A fireplace had been hollowed out in the black tiled walls to warm her feet after she complained about the draft. One evening, she mentioned her fondness for barley porridge sprinkled with cinnamon—a rare spice, even for the gods, but Hades had found it for her. It didn't matter what he placed on that long table stretching out in front of her. Staring at his chiseled, dark features made her sick to her stomach. She couldn't eat a thing.

"How can Earth be in the sky, Hades?" She wished she would never have to say his name again.

"It is a gift for my beautiful bride, who loves the light and warmth of the sun. I tore a hole in the sky of our world so the light of Earth will smile back down at you in all its radiance."

"To remind me that I was kidnapped from my home?"

"To remind you that you are home, and all you desire is yours."

"A gift for your bride, you say—or a show of power because you know my father is coming to take me away from you? Careful, Hades, the river churning around your castle might just overflow with your lies."

Hades rose with a jovial laugh and kissed her forehead. "In less than six months, my beautiful maiden has already bloomed with such strength. You would never have had the courage to speak so boldly to me—or anyone—before. Soon, all your fear will disappear, and you'll learn that you are queen and you can take what you want." His lips grazed her ear.

How is it that his hot breath sends a chill that reaches my soul?

Persephone's gut reaction was to reach for the bread and figs and shove them into her mouth. Somehow chomping on food, stretching out her cheeks, made her feel like she might appear less attractive. She also wanted his comments and his scent that lingered in her memory from their first night together to fade. She couldn't deny what his presence did to her. Sometimes his smooth words and gestures made her doubt the hate that she had for him. But she hated him. She had to remember that.

"Come, my love. There is something I want to show you." His hand heartily swept her away from the sweet breads and he pulled her close to him... too close. But swiftly he turned and led her down the winding halls. Persephone looked up to notice a series of ladders leaning against the walls. Gray spirits perched on top of them with buckets and wooden brushes in their hands. The high halls vibrated with the sounds of the boar bristles brushing back and forth against the hard tiles. But that wasn't what he had wanted to show her. Swiftly he led her to a marble room vastly different from the rest of his dark abode. The floors reflected dozens of white marble columns that stood on either side of a sapphire-blue carpet—a direct path to two thrones. Persephone noticed that the elaborately carved chairs were the same size. Standing before them was a beautiful man clad in a loose-fitting peplos—tunic—and in his hand was an instrument she had never laid eyes on before.

"Poetry and music. Those are the gifts given to this man by Zeus, your father, my love." Hades led Persephone to sit on the elaborate marble depictions of spears and skulls. "They say that if profound bliss could ever be represented in a sound, then it would be the sweet melodies of Orpheus's lyre. Even rocks are said to weep with emotion at the sound of his voice."

His whispers grazed her ears again, bringing her to bite her lower lip.

"Now, he is here in our realm with a very special and unusual request, and I want your wisdom to decide his fate." Hades stepped away.

Persephone felt stiff and formal sitting upright in the cold seat. Even as a goddess, her whole life had revolved around endless fields of flowers whose cushioned blossoms she fell into. A proper chair felt far from her carefree, barefoot days under the sun.

"Please play your music for my wife, Orpheus," Hades said as he left. "I would love to stay myself, but I have a date with another god."

At first, Persephone didn't think she would be moved by the delicate music. She couldn't have anticipated his fluid fingers quivering the strings between the curves of the U-shaped wood. She was startled to hear his voice—sweet and warm. With each vibrato and vibration that danced across the marble walls, she knew she would never be the same.

"Please don't stop!" Persephone hadn't meant to cry out, but she would have given anything to hear one more note.

"I wrote that song for my wife."

Persephone was startled by how much the word *wife* struck a personal chord with her. Was it because Orpheus's face had such a childlike innocence that it felt odd to hear he was a husband?

"She was an Auloniad—a mountain nymph—and she danced through the meadows to this song."

I'd give anything to dance to just one note from this lyre in the meadows of my home.

"You can play here," Persephone swept her arms around the marble room. "Wouldn't you enjoy playing for royalty?"

"Thank you, Your Highness, but I didn't really come here to play in a queen's court."

Persephone bit her lower lip, but this time it wasn't the words of Hades that flushed her cheeks. It was shame. Could a throne hypnotize her ego so much that she could flick her newfound position back at someone? *All the more reason for me to return to my meadows.*

"Why are you here, Orpheus?"

"I want to bring my wife back with me to the world of the living. I came to ask the two of you if I can take her from the underworld."

"You're not…" Persephone's eyes swept over the young man. She hadn't noticed the healthy glow rouging his cheeks. "You're not dead, are you?"

"No, I am not."

"And your… wife. Is she?"

"Yes, unfortunately, that is true."

"Do you love her?" Blushing, Persephone changed her question. "Of course you love her, but what I meant to say was *how* do you know you love her? What is she to you that you would scorch your way to the underworld from the land of the living, tearing up all that is in your path just to have her by your side?"

She paused. She couldn't pretend that her question wasn't about her own fate. But taking her cue, and with a sunny disposition, Orpheus nodded and answered.

"How do I know that I love my wife? How do any of us know what we feel? I know that except for her voice, I have no vigor. She fills me with a sense of awe and wonder and my hands are urged to do wondrous things. You think this music is my fingers playing? No, it is her love that guides them. And if you saw her, you'd know that her smile is pure radiance. It calls on the heat of love, a magic that makes the sanest man go mad with joy."

Persephone's throat felt dry. Orpheus's love rang true. Hades filled her with joy at his doting acts of attention and sadness at… his doting acts of possession. The cursed voice that rang in her ears, cluttering her emotions, couldn't be love.

"Always joy? Does she never bring you sadness?"

Orpheus abandoned his smile. "There are moments when my love and I disagree. It doesn't happen often, but when it does, we always find a way to come back together in love."

With fiery cheeks, she dismissed Orpheus, giving him permission to take his wife back to Earth. Fleeing the throne room, Persephone suddenly felt like the marble columns would crumble under the weight of her heaving chest.

▲▼▲

"But you must have enjoyed his music?"

Hades triumphantly sat across from her at a table laid out with every fine food imaginable. Persephone squinted at him before focusing her eyes on her plate.

"I did."

"Why didn't you have him play here? Didn't I tell you that the desires of your heart—you can have it all? How beautiful a love story it would have been if the lyricist had sacrificed himself to play in the court of the underworld and be with his wife for all eternity?"

Persephone was silent. *Is that what sitting on that throne was supposed to make me feel—that I could take as I pleased?*

"Allowing the dead to return to the land of the living. Does that seem just to you?"

The meal tasted stale to Persephone. The cold, tiled floors seemed to absorb the heat of the fire. And each time she laid her fork down, it clattered like thunder in the silent room. After Hades had left her to decide the fate of Orpheus, he had whisked off to another room to meet with her father. The great god Zeus had made his way down to the underworld himself to have a discussion about his daughter.

Suddenly, Persephone's body didn't even feel like her own. She felt like an object whose fate men could decide. One man swept her away from Earth to make her his bride, while another made a trip away from the blinding light of Helios to make a deal. How could a woman escape the snares of man and create her own fate?

"What did you and my father decide? Will I be able to leave the land of the dead?"

"When I was getting ready to meet with your father, I sought out something that would bring me luck." Hades stood up from the table and reached for a bowl of vibrant red fruit, circular in shape. He fit one into the ball of his hand, and when he cut it open, it burst with bright red juice that spilled out of the soft seeds. Persephone had never seen a fruit so rich.

"I had heard about the pomegranate—it is considered sacred, for those who taste its sweet seeds are provided with abundance, luck, and fertility." Hades bit into the fruit, sending a sea of red spilling into his beard. He wiped his lips and handed the fruit to Persephone. "I ate as much as I could before I went to persuade Zeus of my love for his daughter."

The word *love* reddened Persephone's cheeks with anger. "Enough with your romantic declarations. What did my father decide?"

"We talked a long time, Persephone. He wants to support me as much as he can in finding a wife. But he tells me that your mother, the goddess of fertility, has abandoned all of her life-giving duties in her search for you. Without you, she doesn't care if people starve, drown, or die from ill health. It doesn't matter that I have given you a home filled with more love and loyalty than any other god or mortal could possibly give you. Your mother is clear that you must come home, Zeus said to me."

With a sigh of relief, Persephone suddenly felt her appetite return. Now she was in the mood for succulent fruits. This time, when Hades offered the tiny red pearls, she gladly brought them to her lips. She felt triumphant eating the fruit that must have brought about his misfortune. But as she ate, she noticed that his eyes lingered too long on the seeds staining her lips.

"I want to leave tomorrow."

"And you shall, my love. For several marvelous months, I had you. And I hope you felt similar pleasure in watching yourself blossom and grow." There was something in his eyes that made her remember that first night, when on her back she grabbed tufts of his curls. Within six months, she had become a wife. She had sat on a throne and decided a human's fate. But as she had told him several nights before, she wanted none of it.

"I will see you in the morning for our final good-bye." She turned on her heel to leave the room, but as her eyes caught his, she saw the edges of his lips curl into a familiar smile. *It doesn't matter—hopefully that is a smile that I will leave behind.*

▲▼▲

Persephone's father had already left the underworld to take care of other business. The faithful herald Hermes, whom she often referred to as "Zeus's errand boy," had come to bring Persephone back to Earth. Secretly, she knew it wasn't fair to make light of his role, which was much more important than simply sending messages between Zeus and the other gods. He was the conductor of souls into the afterlife. So he knew Hades and the layout of the underworld well.

"You see, when I first met Hades, your father had entreated me with a new post. I was to be a psychopomp, a guide of souls. So Zen was my disposition, he said, that I would be perfect to escort them to the afterlife. I think your father knew I wouldn't judge them, for that is

Hades's role. There must be a delicate balance understood between the guide and he who judges. You might think that nonjudgmental compassion is all that is required."

Persephone had forgotten how much the beardless youth liked to flex his vocal cords. Speedily, he talked and talked.

"But you must be intelligent too. There is a certain know-how required to avoid being devoured by Hades's guard hound, and you must know what to eat and not to eat."

Persephone blocked out his words as she began her walk away from Hades's abode. Hermes had leapt onto the topic of succulent fruits now. He seemed just as entranced as Hades with the powers of life that the pomegranate was said to bring. He went on and on about the ruby fruit, but Persephone ignored him.

"You didn't eat it?"

Persephone was silent.

"You didn't eat it, did you?"

"What's that? What didn't I eat?"

Hermes's footsteps froze. He turned toward Persephone and grasped her shoulders. "Listen carefully. Do you know what it is I'm saying? Do you understand the severity of this situation? Now, I'll ask you again. Did you eat the pomegranate?"

"The life-giving, lucky red fruit? Hades offered some to me last night."

"Did you eat it? Did you take it?"

"I—yes."

That was the wrong answer. Persephone could see the color drain from Hermes's cheeks.

No one had warned her not to. In fact, she had refused Hades twice before she had eaten the sweet fruit. He had told her it would bring good fortune. *Why is Hermes making such an extravagant fuss about a fruit?*

Standing in the path of the road leading away from Hades's realm, Persephone was surprised to see Orpheus walk by her. Silently, the lyricist passed her, his beautiful lyre tucked under his arm. His lips spread into a smile, then dropped quickly. His steps seemed to move to the beat of some invisible tune, and his eyes were terrifyingly focused straight ahead.

"That's another one that won't make it out of Hades's realm. You need knowledge on not only how to get in and navigate the underworld but also how to get out of it."

"What are you saying to me?" Persephone was exasperated with Hermes's riddles. "I think you need to tell me about the pomegranate and why the lyricist won't leave here."

"Sorry, I misspoke. He will leave here. But she will not." Hermes directed her gaze to a woman climbing the road far behind them. "After you gave Orpheus his wish, Hades made a condition. Orpheus could leave with his wife as long as he did not look behind him before her foot crossed beyond the realm of Hades. If he did look back, she would remain as Hades's forever."

Persephone wasn't entirely sure how this related to her, but she was fearful of the possibility that somehow Hades had made a similar deal with Zeus.

"When you ate the pomegranate, you didn't know you were sealing yourself with a similar fate. When trying to negotiate with your father, Hades did agree to let you leave. But he sure wasn't about to let you go without any conditions. And that rested in the seeds of the pomegranate, a powerful and sacred fruit that ties those who eat its seeds to…"

Hermes didn't have to finish his sentence. Hades had manipulated her. Like the seeds of the earth, she would be tied to the underworld forever. Unflinching, she refused to allow herself to become filled with pity. Instead, she lifted her head high, surveying all that would be her realm.

A beautiful maiden has already bloomed with such strength in six months. Hades's words rang in her ears. *Wait until you see how strong I will become after six months more, Hades. I will take what I want. I will have all of your realm.*

At the end of the road, she could see the high gates shining with such frightening light that few had the strength to cross its threshold and leave. She watched as Orpheus approached the light. His gaze was straight ahead, but slowly, very slowly, it was nakedly obvious that doubt began to overtake him. With his wife so far behind, he wasn't sure if she was coming after all. Persephone watched as his head turned all the way around until his face was clear in the light.

"Oh, Orpheus, you weak-minded fool," she said. But her words weren't directed only toward him.

Persephone's return marked the beginning of spring. Hastening to enjoy the short time that she had with her daughter, Demeter spread her love across the grasses and trees and allowed the earth to ripen with fertility. But when Persephone felt her flesh crawl with thrashing pain, she knew it was time for her to return to the underworld.

"How much I missed the light you bring to my heart. I am thankful to you, Persephone. With you by my side, I am not alone." Hades's love sonnets were just as nakedly desirous of Persephone as they had always been. But Persephone didn't acknowledge her distaste for them. Instead, she ignored them as she ascended her throne."

KALI'S BIRTH

It's not often that the words *mother* and *warrior* go hand in hand. And yet, Mother Durga was popularized in tales as a fierce warrior. Tales of the Hindu goddess showcase her skills combating evil on the battlefield. One such tale involves the "birth" of the goddess Kali, who manifests as an embodiment of Durga's anger.

Samsara—death and reincarnation, the cycle of life in Hinduism—is touched on here. Death is not wholly sad, but accepted as a part of life. Our loved ones' souls may return in a life that is kind to them and may allow us to be with them once more.

"I won't stop fighting for my children. I won't give up. I have the courage to succeed."

If you went onto the battlefield right now and saw the goddess Durga you would see rings of tiredness around her eyes. It wasn't tiredness from the battle itself. No, she enjoyed slicing her enemies into pieces. Her sword was forged from blooms of steel to cut down all that opposed her. Her bow and arrow harnessed her fierce energy. She was the goddess who rode into battle on the great lion, Dawon, whose wide jaw was trained to devour every enemy in her path.

The lines on Durga's face were from the exhaustion of losing. The scent of defeat was new to her—it lingered in the air and permeated her very being.

"Why won't they die?"

It was a scream. It was a protest. She was sick of fighting uselessly. Durga was known as a skilled and powerful fighter. So was her army. But her enemy wasn't following the rules of battle. All she could see for miles were demons—red bodies with gaping mouths multiplying in the distance. *I have lost four thousand men and women since this battle began.*

For months, Durga's armies had been fighting—clashing metal against metal—in the summer heat. Bharata's summers weren't known to be kind. She felt like she was being flayed alive. In a cruel irony, many of her warriors found relief only when they were swept away by the waves of the Sutlej river, their blood tainting its once-blue waters.

But no matter how many of her warriors died, she couldn't handcuff herself to the idea of losing. *What will be the fate of this world if this enemy cannot be contained?* In one hand she held her sword and in her other hand the fear of defeat. *What good is a goddess who can't protect her people?*

Several months ago, her journey onto the battlefield felt like a sure win. In fact, she hadn't expected it to be much of a battle at all.

Mom. I need you. Did she remember the words correctly? There was a village of thatched-roof huts and single-oxen farms in a rainforest clearing just outside of Bharata. Durga loved each and every person who cracked their doors open before sunlight to gather food and water from the earth. Softly, they'd hum to her. There was nothing grand about their worship, like those who offered expensive incense inside Bharata's city walls. But dutifully, every morning the people in this tiny village sang to her.

Mother Durga is the goddess who guides us beyond all confusion to the place of stillness and clarity.

One morning, their tunes turned sour. *Mother Durga! We need you!* In her realm, which mirrored woman and mankind, her vigilant ears heard them screaming. A giant demon was plucking up the villagers one by one and rolling them into a ball to devour. Sometimes, if it had killed too many, it simply tossed the extras into the Sutlej River.

Durga was disgusted. This was the very sort of evil her sword had been forged against. Hearing her children cry out to her was heart-wrenching—*how can a mother not protect her children?* So she set off to slay the demon.

"This will be easy." Her tone was optimistic that day.

"Why do you think so?" A giant paw rose as Dawon smoothed his mane. Not a hair was ever out of place. He slicked a wide pink tongue over his blade-like teeth.

"He's only one demon, however big or brawny. I'm a goddess skilled in the art of battle. Trust me, Dawon, I'll easily defeat him."

"I should come with you." His piercing yellow eyes brought doubt into Durga's mind, weighing on her.

She didn't want that weight. The idea of freedom felt good to her now.

"No, Dawon, this time I want to go alone."

Durga *wanted* to be alone. For centuries, the two had been inseparable. Dawon was loyal to the goddess, following her everywhere she went. They rode into battle together. They ate together. Like a manifestation of her soul, the lion was a wise partner who couldn't be without the goddess. But for the last few years, tension was growing between the two beings. Durga began to realize she didn't even know what the warmth of her own body felt like without Dawon.

So for the first time, and against Dawon's protestations, the two separated. Durga walked into battle alone. After all, it was only one demon. There was no need for a breastplate or armor, let alone her lion. Lazily, she tightened her red sari around her body and allowed her dark curls to fall loosely over her shoulders. All she had in hand was her bow and arrow as she walked along a path that cut through the rainforests to the village. It felt good to see her tiny footprints alone in the moist soil. She breathed in the rich scents of the dense forest cover that still held last night's rain. She could hear her own thoughts. How free she felt amongst the neon and emerald-hued flora that sprang with life around her! Reaching to the heavens, millions of trees stretched to the clouds above her. It felt like everything around her was echoing her newly found sense of freedom.

When Durga came to the end of the path and had the village within sight, she nimbly swung onto the sturdy branches of a tree and perched herself up high. Below, she saw that each door of the thatched-roof limestone homes was shut. On their little plots of lands, cleared for their vegetables, were abandoned oxen still in their harnesses to irrigate the fields. Shattered jugs scattered the water wells. *How dare this demon force my people into hiding!* Preparing her bow and arrow, she peered between shiny, thick leaves. After a few minutes, she spotted the demon, who stood out amongst the bright white buildings and greenery.

So, he's the one who calls himself Raktabīja?

There was something both strong and idiotic about him. He was built broad like a bear, but with a protruding belly. While his teeth were sharpened like swords, his mouth hung open in a wide and silly-looking grin. His red skin shone as brightly as Durga's sari. And his monstrous frame was slow and clumsy, crashing into houses and trees as though his massive shoulders were too heavy for his body.

This will be too easy. Look how big, bright, and loud he is. Look at the softness of his belly. He doesn't even wear armor. My arrow will easily pierce his flesh and kill him. My people will be terrorized no more.

Just for fun, Durga closed her eyes as she shot her arrow past the trees. She didn't need to open them to know that the thud she heard in the distance was his body hitting the ground. But just to be sure—and with her eyes still closed—she shot another arrow. The third time, she turned her back to her enemy and flexed her arms high above her head to shoot the arrow, again without looking. She knew the spot to aim where her enemy would be on the ground. When she heard the last convulsion of his body, she opened her eyes and walked away. She didn't have to look behind her to know that his blood was pouring out.

Regrettably, Durga should have opened her eyes. Then she would have known her enemy was not dead.

The people of the village must have heard the thud too. A door creaked on its hinges. A foot stepped out onto the soft earth. Soon, a few people began to gather the broken fragments of pottery and tend to their oxen. But then there was a change in the air.

"Please, no!" At first it was only one scream. A young woman's shriek faded as a small thud was heard. "There are more of them!" Suddenly, more screams from the village were heard—men and women alike. Some cried for mercy, but the most troubling plea Durga heard was, "Mother, help us!"

The first time Durga became aware of Raktabīja's strange power, she simply thought there were more of this monster—brothers, sisters, or a tribe—he called on before his death. Assuming a small army had arrived, she peered through the trees and shot another arrow. And then another. Four of those burly red demons were shot down. But what she hadn't realized was that every subsequent blow yielded a droplet of blood. And each of those droplets was the seed to a new demon, fully grown within seconds.

Though she had centuries of experience on the battlefield, Durga had been clumsy in her assumption. The enemy was more repellent than she had originally imagined. Winning would require the force of a full army and wisdom from Dawon on how to defeat him.

So on that morning, many months ago, Durga ran back to Dawon and told him all about the demon Raktabīja's ability to replicate himself.

"This is an enemy unlike any we have encountered before. I've heard about some of these demons that have strange powers."

Dawon was more than just a battle-mount of claws and fangs. He was the embodiment of wisdom itself that Durga relied on before every battle.

When Brahma, the creator, called on Durga to destroy Mahishasura—a deceitful shapeshifting demon—it was Dawon who told her the exact moment to strike with her trident. He died mid transformation, when he was at his most vulnerable. And when the ego-hungry King Shumbha and his armies threatened the tranquility of Earth, it was Dawon who knew that no matter how large or powerful they were, the army was only as strong as the leader himself. When she shot her arrow into the heart of the raging king, the million-strong compound of troops dispersed, just as Dawon said they would.

"But how will we defeat this demon?" Despite her resistance, Durga couldn't doubt that the two of them were meant to be together. Did Dawon know she needed his guidance? Could he hear the strain in her voice—a sort of apology—for leaving him alone?

Dawon was silent. The lion didn't lie—that was never effective. Better to be silent than to tell Durga that there were no texts or ancient anecdotes of wisdom about how to kill this demon.

"I will call your armies, and this time we will *all* come with you," Dawon at last replied.

Durga nodded at his words. She read between them closely. There might not be a way for them to win this battle. Still, a mother rises to any occasion where she must protect her children.

Mother Durga, who rouses and orders battle for the people, created Earth and Heaven and resides as their Inner Controller.[5]

It was the chant of her people.

When the lion fully opened his jaw and let his thunderous roar bellow across the known worlds, all the warriors that had served in Durga's armies over the last few centuries heard his call. Without time to spare, Durga and Dawon waited at the edge of the jungle. It didn't take long before the ground shook.

Two thousand war elephants, whose sharpened tusks were trained as spears to slay multiple enemies at once, shook the jungle floor. On their gigantic backs rode a dozen warriors whose aim and skills with arrows were unmatched. Thousands more armored warriors galloped on the backs of horses, each with its own bronze armor. Those who were walking covered their entire bodies—hands, face, legs—in armor. Some said these were the spirits of warriors from the past.

With one roar from Dawon, within minutes, Durga now had an army that was ten thousand men and women strong. But for all the strength and numbers Durga had, what she was missing was wisdom.

Dawon did not have an answer for her. No one had seen anything like this sort of trickery on the battlefield. At first, the lion suggested they kill the demons quickly. Perhaps, if they didn't allow even a second to pass between the time that the demon died and his droplet of blood spilled, there wouldn't be time for the demon to recreate new versions of itself. It was the best plan they had—or at least that's what they believed at the time.

---

5   Ralph T. H. Griffith, *The Rig-Veda* (Santa Cruz, CA: Evinity Publishing Inc., 2009).

Looking back, with the stench of defeat all around her while her enemy multiplied, Durga felt that if she could do it all over again, she would have held her army back. She wouldn't have walked onto that cursed battlefield.

Their loose plan massively failed. So Dawon switched tactics.

"Raktabīja cannot be defeated because each drop of blood creates a new version of himself. And how many droplets of blood do we have flowing within our veins?" Dawon said, scanning the faces of his troops.

Durga's guilt seeped in. "I have called my men and women into a battle they cannot win. My poor people—the earth will surely be swallowed by this bloodthirsty demon," she whispered to her trusted friend.

"We will not lose," Dawon said.

His unwavering strength and reassurance was life-giving to Durga. All she could see was that they were losing this battle. One didn't have to look closely to know that for every one of her enemies she killed, four rose in its place, and then four more for each of those four.

But the lion was persistent in his faith. "The answer will come to us."

Durga knew that Dawon didn't lie. What he said had to be true. And right now, the goddess had to admit that Dawon had brought hope to her. And what hope was left she was able to offer to her warriors.

"These demons multiply from each drop of blood they shed. So do not harm even a single hair on their red skin. Do not kill them!" Durga bellowed to the troops.

Trumpets blasted throughout the battlefield as commanders reiterated her words. Quickly, they sheathed their swords and dropped their arrows to the ground. Now, ropes and nets were the only weapons they carried.

"Wrap them, tie them, disable them. But do not make them bleed!" Dawon roared.

Still, the battle did not go in their favor. How could they tie down a demon, let alone control an army of them? Some of the elephants had been holstered with ropes attached to sturdy nets that captured a few of the demons. But it didn't take long before their sword-like teeth cut through the thick rope. And if the rope—as burly as it was—made even the tiniest cut in the soft red flesh of the demon, each droplet of blood became a new demon. Durga's army couldn't fight them.

Durga tried to help the formations of men and women whose breast-plates were stained from battle. She looked down. She had forgotten to put on her own armor. Her sari—damp with sweat and blood—clung to her skin. Weariness clung to her restless eyes. For months she had heard the names of slain women and men every day. Sometimes she saw the last breath of life drain from their faces. The worst moments were when she received news that an entire flank was swept from the earth. Even so, what was left of her army, those warriors looking up at her, took comfort in knowing they were dying for a worthy cause. But hidden beneath her false valor, Durga admitted to herself she didn't take any comfort in that.

Assisted by the strength of an elephant and twelve warriors, Durga and Dawon were nailing a net full of demons into the damp earth. But elsewhere from the battlefield, one of those grinning red demons had picked up a sword from her own fallen soldiers and was stampeding toward them, his head bobbling back and forth. In what felt like slow motion, Durga saw this silly-looking demon charging toward them with flailing arms.

She could see that there were now more protruding red bellies and gaping sword-like smiles than she had warriors. She could smell her warriors' blood moistening the now-red earth. All around her was the damp stench of death. That stench was coming closer to her with each step of that demon, until he was close enough to raise the sword into the glistening moonlight and bring it right back down into the flesh of Dawon, its tip slicing the lion's heart.

Durga couldn't exactly put into words what Dawon's roar did to her heart. She felt a stinging pain, like a mother whose child is ripped from her womb. Many battles the two had fought together. Dawon's widened jaw would swallow their enemies, and his claws would slice them into pieces. Durga's sword slayed entire armies. But with this demon, they could do nothing. Durga ran to her friend's side. *No!* She cradled his head in her lap. Dawon was more than a friend, more than a brother—he was always by her side. He was like a part of her. She didn't exist without him.

"Breathe," she wailed between sobs. But the lion's soft breaths only faded. "Breathe for me!" The weight of his massive head was sinking deeper into her lap.

Durga's strength was waning. She knew she was meant to pretend she had a never-ending reserve of hope. But how could she maintain hope when she was watching a part of herself die?

All of your caution—how could I have just thrown it to the wind?

Dawon, the lion who had a primal wildness yet was always full of strange fears. He had been so afraid of her walking into battle alone. Now, as night came, Durga became terribly scared of the darkness as Dawon took one last fragile breath. The lion was too weak to say good-bye.

"Please don't leave me! I don't want to be alone now!" The burden of her choice noiselessly crushed her heart as his blood soaked into her already wet clothes. In that second, when she saw the most important being in her life fade from this earth, a new emotion flashed within her—bloodthirsty rage.

"Enough with this madness!" No, this would not be her story. "I created all worlds at my will, without any higher being, and permeate and dwell within them. The eternal and infinite consciousness is I, it is my greatness dwelling in everything."[6]

If Dawon couldn't devour Raktabīja and her sword couldn't slice him, then she, Mother Durga, would create a being who could defeat this foul, blood-replicating demon. In the light of the full moon, she absorbed the night's energy. On the red battlefield, she drew the darkness to her and began her work. Until now, no one had been able to create a plan or find a weapon that could defeat him. But she, Mother Druga would.

As one of the demons came close to her, she kicked it in its belly. It then went waddling in a different direction.

"Roar with delight while you still can, O illiterate demon, because when I will kill you, the gods themselves will roar with delight."[7]

In the darkness she outlined the curves of a woman. Durga carved her strong, long legs. She shaped her breasts. Her shoulders would be broad. She plucked stars from the sky for her bright, wild eyes. With the seaweed that washed onto the shores of the Sutlej River, she strung together strands of wavy hair. And with the blood from one of the demons, she painted the being's lips. Much like herself, this being had the form of a beautiful woman, but there was something more terrifying about her. She held a purpose outside of child bearing or protecting her people. She would be a devourer.

Durga shaped her tongue to be long and lolling. Her multiple arms could hold an army of weapons, but Durga gave her only one—a khatvanga, a staff that she topped with the head of one of the demons. In the light of the moon, she clothed her with a skirt made from

---

6   Griffith, *The Rig-Veda.*
7   Kyle Tortora, *Legends of Hindu Goddess Durga: The Invincible,* https://www
.lotussculpture.com/blog/hindu-goddess-durga.

the breastplates of her fallen men. She draped only a garland of red flowers around her neck to cover her breasts.

"Wake up, my beautiful creation," Durga softly sang. She didn't quite know what she would name the being. But the name would come to her.

"She who is black." She sang about the being's onyx skin. "She who devours time." She sang about the being's long tongue and wide mouth. "Divine Mother Kali." Finally, the name came to her. "Bloodthirsty you will be."

When she swept her hands over the being's eyes, they opened and Kali breathed with life. Her purpose was clear. Durga didn't have to say why she had been made. Her lips were painted with blood, and that is what she craved. The bright, wide eyes went searching for it.

Wildly, the being crawled along the battlefield and licked up every droplet of Raktabīja's blood. She swept her long tongue over the damp earth and sucked blood out of it. If a droplet fell onto the body of a fallen warrior, she sucked that dry too. But it wasn't only the demons' blood that she devoured—thousands of the red demons populated the battlefield, and Kali did what Durga's armies could not. She devoured those hordes of demons and caught the blood of each before it could fall to the ground, stopping him from creating more duplicates.

Durga watched as her creation swept over the battlefield. Sometimes, it felt good to allow someone else to fight. It allowed her to focus on another task—that of healing. She dug her hands in the blood-soaked soil and sprinkled it over the lion's closed eyes. There wasn't time to bathe and wrap her dear friend. But she would ensure that his soul would have peace and his physical body would return to the earth. *"May your spirit return again to perform pure acts for exercising strength, and to live long and to see the sun."*[8]

---

8   Griffith, *The Rig-Veda.*

She looked up. Kali had swallowed all of Raktabīja's duplicates until finally, only the original one was left. So daft was this demon that he didn't try to run or hide. Just as Durga had observed in the village, he stumbled around as though his head was too big for his massive body. He stumbled into Kali and would have trampled the new being. But Kali did what Kali was created to do—she opened her mouth wide and consumed.

We're victorious? It was half a question of disbelief and half a declaration of joy. *What creature is this that I have created—the manifestation of my anger that has the ability to do what no one in this army could do?*

Slowly, she rose to her feet. Without Dawon, she would have to direct her own watchful gaze to steadily observe and question what she saw around her. The new being was effective at defeating Raktabīja on the battlefield. But something about her worried Durga. A crazed look of bloodlust shone in Kali's eyes. And she wasn't sure if this being—built only for the purpose of bloodlust—could be fully trusted to control herself. *But she will be a story I will worry about another day.*

The demon Raktabīja and all his replicates had been fully devoured by Kali. The battlefield was quiet. The women and men who bravely endured and fought by her side for months could now rest. But having lost so much, a scent of defeat hung about them despite their final triumph. And having fought for so long, their bodies were shaken and sore. As the sun rose over their victory, Durga walked along the flanks of warriors, thanking each one.

"Dawon—where is he?" she heard again and again.

"We have lost the wisest and most powerful among us!" Durga cried out to the crowd. "Let that be how we remember them! Think of their moments of courage, their valor, their honor, and their words of wisdom that guided and directed you to victory!"

Tears blurred Durga's vision. She hadn't meant for her speech to be about Dawon, but as she spoke, she realized that like a flood, her emotions couldn't be contained. She couldn't speak anymore. Some victories don't come without a loss, and what she lost on that day was perhaps the most important part of her.

Candles were lit on the battlefield to honor the dead, and smoke rose as their bodies were burned—sent back to the earth that had originally given them life.

Mother Durga is the goddess who guides us beyond all confusion to the place of stillness and clarity.

Maa Durga is the protector of mankind, as she is the figure of a mother, always ready to protect her child.

In the distance, Durga could hear the chants of her people. Their simple songs were rising with the sun as they began their morning rituals. Today, all those who had called on Mother Durga would be safe. The goddess was victorious. Perhaps all was as it should be.

MAMAN BRIGITTE

Death is inevitable. It is a path that every person must face. In Voodoo, it is the loas, or spirits, that guide humans from this world to the afterlife. The most powerful loas are Baron Samedi and Maman Brigitte. Humans who live a good life are nurtured by their guidance to the land of the dead. But rest assured, those who violate others or live a life of greed and violence will be avenged by the loas. Welcome to the underworld of New Orleans.

Coupled with folklore about powerful spirits is the real-life story of a prostitute—the Storyville Slayer—who was known to kill men who harassed or abused her fellow prostitutes. She first made headlines in 1856 and was last heard of in 1861, when she was released from prison after a yearlong sentence.

*Content warning: this story contains depictions of rape.

A tinge of purple lined the horizon. It wouldn't be long before the black rooster called for the sunlight to come, chasing away all that was dark and hidden in the night. Maman Brigitte took another swig of her spiced rum. It was a shame morning was coming so soon, because she loved the balmy nights in New Orleans.

She loved how the night welcomed celebrations, boisterous with laughter and overflowing drinks. Her husband, Baron Samedi, could throw a party like no other, where beautiful people danced until they stumbled into the morning sun. She loved seeing her husband's face in candlelight—flickers of lust drove him to grab her breasts and penetrate her against a wall for raucous lovemaking.

Again Brigitte brought the sweet liquor to her lips. She dug her toes into the soft earth. She would get back to tonight's party soon and again make love to her husband. But for now, she needed to feel the cool air of the night. She needed the moonlight to dance across her bare skin between the slits of her purple skirt.

Softly humming to herself, Brigitte played with the grass between her toes. She leaned against a large gray stone while notes of rich spices floated up to her. She was loved here. Her people honored her—the loa of the dead—for healing the sick and guiding the dead into the afterlife. She was feared here too. Few were so foolish as to provoke her anger. Knowing the joy she took in sweet liquors, rum was left for her on the graves of elders.

She was about to take another sip when a sound disturbed her. It was hushed and muffled, but she could tell there were people here amongst the graves. Gingerly she walked toward the sounds rustling the leaves.

"Please, no," called out the voice of a young woman. Her slurred words were followed by the limp pounding of her fists.

"Quiet, woman! Is this not what you wanted when you were tantalizing me with your flesh?" A man's voice boomed into the night. "Besides, no one can hear you out here."

The woman cried. The man snorted and huffed.

Brigitte was disgusted. *Well, it seems that some are unwise enough to rouse my anger.*

She could see the two of them clearly now. Hiding in the shadows against a tree, his pants half down, the man pinned the young woman to the ground, lifting up her skirts. Brigitte didn't have to question what had happened moments before. The woman's eyes were flickering almost as if she were fighting sleep.

Against her will, this man had brought her to his place. Now, he is desecrating the resting place of his ancestors as he is desecrating this woman.

The attack didn't last long. The man got up and left. The woman was left limp in the dirt, crying and trying to cover herself with her skirts.

"Don't cry, child," Brigitte whispered as she knelt down, lowering the woman's skirts to her knees. "That f***ing man will pay. Maman Brigitte is here for your revenge. Marked him I have for misery. His d*** will fall off for hurting you, child. His days of peace will be no more. And when his miserable days are gone, you will s*** on his grave."

The rooster crowed. Brigitte could feel the warmth of dawn approaching, painting the night sky with hints of cornflower blue. Soon, the night would be no more.

"I must leave now, child." Soothingly she stroked the woman's head. "But fear not. Be consoled that the loa of death will avenge you."

Tossing the last of the rum down her throat, Brigitte felt a new fire fill her flesh: bloodthirsty revenge. One of her followers had been violated. She left footsteps in the damp soil as she disappeared into the night.

Those knowledgeable of Voodoo are aware that death is only the beginning. Our bodies might turn to dust in this world, but our spirits continue on in a realm side by side with the human world. Called Guinee, this land of the spirits is accessible only through gates protected by loas. Scattered throughout the French Quarter are these seven gates, called the "Gates of Guinee." Loa can pass through easily enough, but woe to the living who should come too close, for these gates separate the living from the dead.

Brigitte stomped through the streets of Guinee. The spirit realm looked almost the same as that of the living. The tall grasses of the Bayou gently swept across her legs. A canopy of trees danced with the stars overhead. But here, the beautiful moon shone every hour of the day. Sometimes it rose and fell in the sky, but it was always there. At this hour, the moon was high as Brigitte marched her way through the cobblestone streets to the mansion she shared with her husband.

"Baron!" Brigitte's voice echoed through the streets. "Where is my husband? Bar-r-ron!" The r's harshly rolled off her tongue.

Whiffs of tobacco levitated in the air. Ah, yes, she had only to follow the scent of cigars and rum to find her husband, whose bony fingers would be wrapped around his treasured glass of liquor. Thankfully, as she mounted the steps to their mansion, it was quiet. Had the party moved back to their residence, Brigitte would have been less than thrilled to partake in more lascivious festivities. Nor was she in the mood to swat away silly mortals smitten with the mysteries of her husband and the spirit realm.

"Bar-r-ron!"

Roaming the wide halls, she stopped at a drawing room in the west wing when she spied his black top hat lounging on the corner of a purple velvet couch. He was never without his top hat. It paired well with his black coattails and patent leather shoes. All in all, his black-tie attire made his tall frame even more attractive.

"Master of the Dead, we have a problem! One of my followers has been violated."

Brigitte sank into a chair opposite her husband. A fire roared next to her. Somehow, its warmth smoothed her emotions, allowing her thoughts to flow into a plan instead of remaining as unmoored anger. She twirled the ice in her glass as she poured herself a new drink.

"I saw it with my own eyes." She took a gulp to ease her temper. "A man took a woman to the graves and violated her. I saw her tears. And you know what he said? He told her that no one could hear her. Well, I heard her cries. Now vengeance boils through my veins. No woman should live in fear of a man. No man should be able to force himself on a woman!"

The drink was gone now, and Brigitte filled her glass again to the brim. Baron watched his wife shake with emotion, spilling her liquor.

"I'm sorry for what your eyes have seen this night." Tenderly, Baron reached out to hold his wife's hand. For a second he held her, sharing her sadness.

But he couldn't help but trace the outline of his wife's curves in the firelight. It was tempting, the way her blouse fell off her shoulders and the corset pushed up her bosom. God, she was beautiful. Her flaming red curls were as wild as her passion. And when it came to her people, all of the spirits and loas spoke of her never-ending devotion to her followers. Her vengeance against anyone who harmed them was legendary. Baron had never met anyone as devoted and fierce. Even when she was angry, when she breathed heavily like this, she was wildly attractive.

He leapt back into his usual playful manner. The job of loas shouldn't disrupt his fun. "You should have been with me enjoying the party, my love. If it bothers you too much, let me take revenge on this man. I will ensure he gets what he deserves. And then, my dear, we'll celebrate!"

"No!" Brigitte rose and stood before the fire. "What kind of loa would I be if I didn't seek vengeance for my followers, but passed it on to my husband? The woman is devout; she brings gifts and prayers to her grandmother's grave. I reckon tomorrow she will be there offering up her prayers of revenge. And I will be there to fulfill her wishes!"

"The man—I've seen him about town. What he follows, I know not. But I do know one thing. He is rich."

Sulking in his chair, Baron puffed heavily on his cigar. He knew that voice. His wife's mind wouldn't be changed. Best to help her find a resolution quickly so he could get back to enjoying life.

"And what revenue do you think is fitting for such a crime, my love? Possession? I could take over his body and make him drink at a bar until he confesses to his crimes. How much do you think this mortal could drink? It's been so long since I have truly been drunk." The fire reflected in Baron's eyes.

"My husband. Strong drinks and parties!" Her glass was empty again. Annoyed, Brigitte placed it on the table. She had no desire to fill it again. She knew her husband all too well. It wasn't her follower he cared about.

She left the room. Her mind was too ill at ease to make any decision at the moment; all she could do was anxiously pace the halls.

The man I saw this night has no respect for the living or the dead. Making him confess, that's a plan I like. But is that enough? I want him to feel as horrified as the woman he violated. I want him to feel terror between his loins and call to the gods for help! I want him to beg for mercy!

Hours passed as Brigitte's mind swirled with thoughts and her footsteps paced the halls. Soon, daylight was fading in the human world, and a dark fog rose from the bayou, shrouding the graves.

"Maman Brigitte."

The words were barely audible at first. But Brigitte could hear her name whispered from a mouthful of tears. Leaving the mansion, she followed the sound to the same graveyard she had been to earlier. Kneeling beside a tombstone was a woman laying out treats from a basket at the base of the tomb—sweet peppers, spiced rum, and candles.

"Maman Brigitte. Please! I call on your great and powerful name! Many women have been wronged by an influential man. I look to you for vengeance, and I ask you for freedom!"

Shivering in the damp night air, the woman pulled her shawl over her shoulders as she knelt to pray. She didn't care that the hem of her white dress and her delicate silk slippers were becoming tarnished with mud.

"Loa of death. Forgive me, but I hate my husband. Last night, at these very graves that you watch over, I saw him as he forced himself upon a woman. But I shouldn't say that she is just a woman. She is my maid, whom I brought into my home to give safety, a warm bed, and a life outside the streets of Storyville. And she had that. She was going to be married this spring to a sweet man who could provide for her and, most of all, love her. But my husband has taken that away from her, just as he takes from all women."

The woman lifted her face to the moon. What should have been eyes shining bright were swollen black and violet. Her lips, too, were swollen, and Brigitte could see nicks of blood where her skin had come in contact with something sharp. Still, the woman raised her head with a quiet dignity. She had perfectly combed and coiffed her hair. She had even put on pearls that dangled from her ears.

"How can I endure being married to such a cruel man? Obediently I tended to our estate, ensuring that my husband was comfortable and would not be dishonored by me. I gave birth to our son. And even when it became apparent that he didn't love me, quietly I turned my back when he took on many mistresses. Many nights I've endured his fists when his temper was rallied by strong drinks. But I cannot endure any more. Maman, I beg you, spare me and my child from this man, and take vengeance on him so we may have our freedom."

Voices in the distance startled the woman. Swiftly, she blew out the candles and wrapped the shawl around her head, covering her hair and shielding the swollen parts of her face. She lifted her hands to her throat and fidgeted for a moment with the clasp of her necklace.

"Remember me, Maman. My name is Celine," she said, laying the necklace on the tombstone. With light steps she quickly left the graveyard.

The voices didn't come any closer, but faded into the distance, leaving Brigitte alone. The moon shone high as the winds rustled the leaves overhead.

The woman knew her well. The rum she'd left was one of her favorites. Taking a swig, she picked up the necklace. It was a fine piece indeed. A strand of freshwater pearls dipped into a cross entirely composed of amethysts. Few families in New Orleans could afford one of these stones, let alone enough of the lustrous gems to make a dazzling cross. A symbol of the woman's wealth and her devout faith now rested in Brigitte's hands.

So this man has wronged more than one woman. Mark my words. Tonight will be the worst night of that man's life.

Brigitte clasped the necklace around her own throat. She devoured the peppers and carried the bottle of rum as she set out into the night to find the malicious young man. She had accepted Celine's sacrifice. Now a fire of vengeance roared through her body.

It wasn't difficult to find the man. Celine had already told Brigitte so much. A man of exorbitant wealth in New Orleans had the finest restaurants, theaters, and bars at his disposal. But when combined with a lust for beautiful women, well, any man with passion in his loins and a lack of virtue in his heart couldn't help but be drawn to the red-light district: Storyville. There, the cobblestone streets came alive at night when the most beautiful women offered their services to men willing to pay a pretty gold coin or two.

Amongst all the women vying for coins to be dropped into their laps, one woman in particular stood out who had no trouble getting the attention of drunk men seeking a warm embrace for the night. This woman was wanted above all others in Storyville, especially amongst rich men. Her name was Delia Swift. And she could be found at the famed speakeasy, Belle Époque.

Maman Brigitte stomped into the venue. The bar was loud with laughter from men having liquor poured into their mouths by women clad in little more than corsets and stockings. A piano somewhere kept the atmosphere light with fast-paced tunes. Toward the back, thick velvet curtains were drawn over the stage.

Delia had yet to dance. The prized whore of Storyville liked to make her patrons wait, sometimes refusing to go on until well past midnight. Sometimes, gold coins would be thrown onto the stage to urge her to come out. But Delia did as she pleased, when she pleased. When she did take the stage, the venue was quiet as she captivated the men with her erotic dance of feathers and bare legs. If they were lucky, she might be in the mood to give a quick flash of her breasts.

Brigitte walked to the back of the stage. She slipped into Delia's dressing room. The woman was alone, counting the thing she loved the most—money. No doubt it was from last night's admirer. And no doubt she'd have more to count tonight, for even Brigitte admitted that the young woman was beautiful. Like herself, Delia had a halo of wild, flaming-red curls that flowed over smooth shoulders sloping into the most graceful body in all of Storyville. Those curls were famous amongst the men who visited the red-light district. They both loved and feared the rich color.

Rumors swirled of a gang of red-headed women who took vengeance on men who wronged the whores of Storyville. If a man was seen hitting a whore, it wasn't out of place for his body to be found facedown in the river the next day. But no evidence was ever found to convict the women.

Maman Brigitte whispered a few words of magic that allowed her to be seen by Delia. A gasp left the woman's lips at the sight of her.

"Don't be afraid, child," she said. "I am here not to harm you, but to see if we might help one another. I am Maman Brigitte, a loa of the dead. One of my followers has been harmed by a man who I have no doubt will be here to see you perform one of these nights. He is a rich man with a wife named Celine."

"Oh, I know him, all right," Delia sighed. "I don't bother myself with knowing the names of too many wives, but that family is one of the three richest in town. And that man is one of the most hated too. The wife's a sweet one though. She took a beating when she came looking for her husband the other night. She's the only wife I've ever apologized to. It was awful the way her man beat her like that. But I tried to tell her, I's gotta eat, honey."

"You felt compassion for this woman—so then, will you take revenge on him in my name? I'll tell you exactly what to do to the man. In return, I promise you protection. No man will harm you, and you will be found innocent of your crimes."

Delia was quiet for a second. Slowly, she spoke. "You know what kind of woman I am. I gotta eat, and sex is money, honey. If word got out that I take revenge for being wronged, well—the money would dry up like that." She snapped her fingers for a dramatic effect before continuing. "I myself might even be beaten for rumors like that.

"I've seen all kinds of men out there. But in the bedroom I know how to manage them, so that's where I like to keep them. And women like me don't believe in loas or nothing. Even now, I believe more in these gold coins here than I do you."

A crooked smile crossed Brigitte's lips. She walked over to Delia. "Believe in this." Swiftly, the necklace left her throat and fell into the woman's hands. "You believe in loyalty. That I know, or else the men wouldn't whisper stories of a gang of women avenging those who have been hurt by their drunken patrons. Now, I ask you to protect your fellow women. Last night that man violated a woman at my graves who was once from Storyville. She is his maid now. You will help me exact my revenge. Follow my instructions, and bring Celine's husband to the gates of Guinee. I will do the rest. Then you leave this place and find a new life, child, because with this necklace you'll have enough gold to eat well forever."

With these words, Maman Brigitte's form faded. She could no longer be seen by the mortal.

▲▼▲

The *Times Picayune* said: "*It is an old game, and the young gentleman, Andre Damas, has paid dearly as many before him have for seeing the 'elephant' (living life to the fullest, no matter the risk).*"

So, his name is Andre. Brigitte said to herself. Somehow when the spirit had wandered naked and wounded into the spirit world, she had forgotten to ask him his name.

"Baron!" She yelled for her husband at the sight of the new spirit. "Our prisoner is here."

In typical fashion, her husband met her at the graves with puffs of smoke swirling up to his top hat. In his other bony hand he clasped his glass of rum. But instead of being playful and full of fun, his eyes were lit with a terrifying fire.

"This man has lived a life exploiting those weaker than him. Now it is the season of revenge. Show him just how horrible Guinee can be to the wicked."

Turning to the spirit, she said, "There is no promise of heaven here. There is only darkness. And you will be taken to the darkest corner of them all, where you will live a million years of tormented gnashing of your teeth and crying—that is, if we let you keep your teeth and eyes."

A few days later, the town was buzzing with news of the murder of one of the richest men in New Orleans. His naked body was lying at the entrance of one of the cemeteries. The coroner said the man had had some sort of shock that sent his heart into a fit—he wasn't sure if that was before or after he had been stripped. Interestingly enough, the killer had also chosen to perform a sort of surgery. It appeared that a mixture of salt and crushed ice had been used to effectively castrate the man of his testicles and penis.

It was no wonder that the good men of New Orleans were terrified by this violent crime. Worst still, no suspect could be found. Who *didn't* hate Andre Damas enough to kill him? The merchants he ripped off? Everyone knew that when his wife didn't show up at the season's latest ball, she was nursing a swollen eye from one of her husband's latest tirades. Even the mayor was relieved his greatest patron and blackmailer was gone. So instead of focusing on finding the killer, the papers took a different angle.

"Let this murder be a lesson to our good city. If we don't seek the moral cover of the good Lord and leave these lustful extravagances behind, then surely our society is going to fade away. Men must live straight to shoot straight."

Indeed, the city did begin to change. The newly widowed and exceedingly rich Celine Damas purchased several buildings in the red-light district and turned them into warehouses for her new business, where she imported luxurious fabrics from France. Several of the townsmen who purchased their suits and coats from Celine recognized her employees as women from an old life they quietly hid from their wives.

Maman Brigitte noticed that more of these men began to leave rum, sweet peppers, and candles on the graves for her husband. They had more time on their hands to devote to religion now that the red-light district was swiftly changing into a merchant port. Their prayers and hymns were a sweet tune that she loved to dance to with her Baron.

"There is a house in New Orleans they call the rising sun…" Softly, Maman Brigitte whispered into her husband's ear as they danced into the violet horizon. How much she loved the balmy nights of New Orleans.

SHINIGAMI'S CANDLE

From the moment we take our first breath, death becomes our only guarantee. So why should it be feared? In Japan, ancient views of the afterlife are chronicled through Shintoism and Buddhism, both of which share the ethos of death being a part of the circle of life, nothing more and nothing less.

It was around the eighteenth century, during the Edo period, that Western influences brought about a new view of death and sparked a series of "scary fables" much like we have in the West. One of the most popular of these stories involves the Shinigami. *Shi* stands for "death" while *kami* is "god" or "spirit." This version of a Grim Reaper first appeared as death spirits that take humans to the afterlife or possess them into taking their own lives. But in keeping with the idea that death is merely a part of life, people are taken by a Shinigami only when their candle, or lifespan, is finished—never before and never after. What sets this legend of death apart from other Japanese ideas of death is that, depending on the Shinigami, these spirits can either become monsters or helpers.

*Content warning: this story contains depictions of someone thinking about suicide.

"I tried!" Kame screamed into the cool air. "I tried." Tears blurred his vision as he wailed. At age thirty-seven, this was it for him. "I'm going to see you soon, my love," he whispered as a feeling of calmness came over him.

This was what he wanted his last words to be before he saw his wife again. Kame wasn't a man who usually wanted to talk about his wife, or even think about her, for that matter. He was sick of thinking about her—literally. He could not get out of bed without hearing her footsteps on the creaky wooden floorboards of their cottage. He didn't want to eat without her laughter and the sweet aroma of the congee she cooked, warming their home. So most mornings he did not get out of bed. He covered his ears to block the sound of the outside world. He barely touched the parcels of steamed buns or tofu his neighbors left on his doorstep. This was the theme of his life now. Kame was practically the walking dead himself.

Now, as he stood on the edge of the bridge looking down at the harsh waters, he realized he wanted to leave this life behind.

He had woken up that morning with an urge to leave his dark cottage but no knowledge exactly of where his feet would take him. Without any aim or goal, he squinted from the sunlight that seemed foreign to him after spending months holed up at home. His getas—wooden thong sandals with high-teethed soles that took some getting used to again when he hadn't worn them for months—tripped on the granite rocks that lined the roads. It was as if the universe was reiterating what his place was in this world—a blundering man who had no real strength or purpose outside of the love a beautiful woman had once given him. Perhaps that's why his feet quickly walked away from his home and village toward the long bridge that led to the mainland.

Every day during the summer, he and his wife would come and sit on this bridge to eat sweet dumplings while the sun set over their village.

"I love our Sato-umi so," she'd wistfully say, biting into the sticky buns stuffed with bean paste.

This Sato-umi—small coastal village—was neatly tucked between a range of tree-covered mountains and the Ine Bay. The wooden homes looked like they could come alive, she said, because they rested on stilt-like structures that mimicked legs. *And do you see the way the windows and doors are placed? They're in the same positions as our eyes, nose, and mouth.*

As Kame and his wife dangled their feet like children, dusk would turn into night and they'd giggle together, making dirty jokes about made-up constellations that they swore they saw in the sky.

"I love our Sato-umi too," Kame would say before they walked home hand in hand.

Now, from his perch on the bridge, he noticed how tiny the fishermen looked along the rocky shores as they packed up their belongings and catch of the day from their local beach market. Laughing to himself, he realized his wife had been right. The fishermen looked like small morsels of rice running into the mouths (the doors) of the "living houses."

"Watashitachi no mura o fakku," Kame said as he stared at the wooden huts lining the granite shore. Today, he f****** hated this village. This had been true ever since his wife died. Nothing quite seemed the same without her.

"The way of medicine is solely through chu and sei."

These were the first words the doctor said when he knelt beside Kame's wife on that awful night. Pulling out a small wooden box of tools, he struck Kame with a long, odd-looking needle. Kame didn't understand why the doctor had given medicine to him and not his wife.

"Medicine has its limits. There is nothing left for me to do but inoculate the healthy. She is too far along in the sickness, so we must help her accept death with dignity," the doctor said calmly.

Why didn't the doctor consult his medicinal textbooks? Weren't there herbs he could have given her from his bag? This is why my wife died. They told me she was sick and no one could help her. Instead, the doctor gave medicine to all of the healthy people in the village.

Kame laid his body out flat on the long wooden bridge. He had forgotten that he hadn't left his house in months. His legs were a narrow strip of muscle now. Even his yukata felt heavy on his shrunken frame. It was odd, considering that the thin piece of cotton cloth didn't even have a lining. As he lay there, staring up at the red sky beyond the green mountains, he smiled, thinking this would be the last sunset alone without his wife. Why were couples joined to spend life *together*, only for one person to leave the other? He felt like the spirits hadn't put much thought into unions and vows of marriage.

"It is best if we go together," he said to himself as he rolled up to his feet.

Kame spread his arms wide and stepped over the edge of the bridge. What were a few minutes of pain to end the years of suffering life had brought him? But—instead of feeling his body crash into the waves below, there was nothing. Kame opened his eyes. Was he dead already?

No. He hadn't even left the bridge. Something was holding him back, and suddenly that something gave a strong yank. Losing his balance, he fell backward with a thud. Rubbing a hand against his hurt skull, Kame scrambled to his feet.

"Seishin?!" Kame stuttered at the being standing in front of him. Shaking, he tried to leap again from the bridge. Better to be a dead man than to let a seishin—spirit—possess his body. But before he could make another attempt, the seishin yanked him back.

"Seishin, please do not possess my body!" Kame yelled. "Look at me. I am a weary man," he pleaded.

Didn't the spirit see how his clothes hung off his frame, emaciated from spending days in bed? Didn't he see how thin his hair was from the stress of loss? Or how tired his hollow cheeks looked from months of unfulfilling sleep?

The seishin nodded. For a second, the massive spirit didn't say anything. Instead, the seishin's nine-foot frame—also emaciated—sulked over Kame, who doubted that its wide yellow eyes could hold an ounce of intelligence. There was something unsettling about that pale white face. Perhaps it was because the eyes didn't blink? Or maybe it was the mini-knife-like teeth that never closed from its wide grin?

At last the seishin spoke. "Weary you are. Possessed you won't be, or dead either. I am a Shinigami, a death spirit. I choose who lives and dies. It is not yet your time."

"I don't understand," Kame said.

"You want to end your life by throwing your body off this bridge. I am here to tell you that it is not your time to die."

"Not my time," Kame repeated. "But seishin, surely you know the story of my life. I have nothing left to live for." Kame rose to his feet again. "I have made my decision. Now, let me die honorably instead of living miserably."

The large seishin leaned over Kame. "Your time has not yet come. Each human life is like the flame of a candle. When you are born, the flame is lit. But as time goes on, the wax burns until the final flame turns to ash. Your candle has not finished burning."

"But what am I to do with this miserable life?" Tears began to fall down Kame's face.

"The way of medicine is solely through chu and sei. Do you know what that means, Kame?"

How dare he. The first, last, and only time that Kame had heard that phrase was from the doctor who told him to accept the death of his wife. Now the Shinigami was saying the same words to Kame, but this time asking him to accept life.

"I will tell you a secret, Kame, that will ease your pain."

"Now that you have seen me, you will be able to see other Shinigami. We arrive when a human is close to death. Whether or not that person's time has come will determine where a Shinigami positions himself—either at the feet or the head of the person."

"Is that why you were at my feet, yanking me backward?" Kame huffed.

The Shinigami nodded. "Yes. Your flame is still burning, and it is not your time to die. So I will give you a gift. You will be allowed to see not only myself but all Shinigamis."

Kame stared blankly as the words left the giant seishin's mouth. Why would he want to see other Shinigamis? A tall white spirit, clothed in black, with sharp teeth in an eternal grin—seeing that was terrifying. *What life is that?*

"Now when I leave here, you must walk to the other side of this bridge and down the dirt road to the right. Follow it. There will be a house with a sakura tree that grows by the front door. Knock on that door and tell them you are there to heal their son. When their son is well, ask them to pay you a doctor's fee."

Kame violently shook his head. "Perhaps this gift is better suited for another man." His eyes drifted over the sunset and then at the waters below. *Don't worry. I will be with you soon, my love.*

For a while the seishin was quiet, staring at Kame with that terrifying knife-like grin.

"How odd it is that you lack understanding about how desperate the living are to avoid death and how much they're willing to pay to save those they love. This sunset is beautiful, but it won't be your last. You will see many more. And you will see many Shinigami at the feet of the sick. When you see them, whisper the words *Sōde wanai*. They will leave, and the person will be healed. If the Shinigami is at the head, leave that person be and do not take any money from the family. This gift is yours, Kame. Remember to use it wisely. The way of medicine is solely through chu and sei."

Perhaps if I walk to the other end of this bridge, this spirit will leave me alone. So Kame did just that. He plastered a smile on his face as he began to walk silently across the bridge. When he turned to look behind him, the seishin was gone.

Kame had to admit that the bridge to the mainland was long. And this was the first time he was walking across it. Or was it? He couldn't remember if he had walked across as a child. But as an adult, he had to stop several times to rest before he got to the other side. The moon was high in the sky by the time he reached it. Kame knew that no one would be out on the bridge at this hour of the night. It was the perfect time to continue his original mission. And with no Shinigami around, he readied his feet at the edge of the bridge.

But as he looked out at the dark line of trees before him—speckled with lights from the neighboring village—he became intrigued. He had never been to the mainland and was mesmerized wondering what the people on this side were like. This wasn't a remote fishing village, and there were no houses on legs nestled between the mountains and rocky shores. The road that led from the bridge seemed to cut straight through their large town. It was made from neat rows of wooden planks—so different from the dirt roads he was used to. A series of wooden houses—strikingly different from what he was used to—lined both sides of the road. Bright lights shone from these homes as townspeople stood on balconies. In and out of doors, people left and returned. *What are they doing?* Without him realizing it, his feet went down this path.

"What are you doing?" a villager said to him. The man looked foreign to Kame. His yukata was tied differently, with a wide belt at his waist. Even his hair was tied into an elaborate bow style on top of his head. It was the single-braid style that made it easy for the people of his village to place a straw hat over.

"I'm searching for a house with a sakura tree at the end of a dirt road." Startled, all that Kame could think to say in reply was what the Shinigami had told him. *After all, I might as well see what the Shinigami's riddle was all about.*

The villager's eyes widened, then seemed to sink back into a pool of sadness. Without a word, his just as swiftly walked through the wooden streets until he stopped outside of a wooden building that had hundreds of pink blossoms dusting its doorstep. Kame could tell it had been a long time since anyone had swept there. The wooden lattice made it difficult to peer inside, but Kame could hear the words softly mumbled to the people inside. "Isha is here," the villager said.

Doctor? Me?

The smell of sickness was instantly recognizable when the heavy lattice doors slid open. It hung like a pungent fog that seemed to mute everyone's speech. The man and woman of the house slid open a door in the hallway. Inside the small room was a young boy resting on a shikubuton—a thin cotton mattress—on the floor. He couldn't have been more than ten. Maybe, he was thirteen, because his features were so emaciated that he looked smaller. All that Kame knew was that the boy was too young to die. Hanging on the walls around his head were the same red watercolor paintings that Kame had been given when his wife was sick.

"This disease comes from an onryō, a type of seishin that seeks vengeance," an elderly fisherman had told him. After listening to her symptoms—a headache, pain throughout her body, the inability to hold down her food, and small red dots multiplying on her skin—villagers suggested the only way to heal her was to hang a red watercolor painting to appease the evil seishin of housou, the disease they believed his wife had.

Kame didn't ask what disease the boy had. Hovering at his feet was a Shinigami with the same jagged smile as the one Kame saw on the bridge. *Was a Shinigami there when my wife died too?* Kame wondered.

Boldly, he raised his voice. "No one is going to die tonight," he said, staring straight into the wild yellow eyes of the seishin.

"Sōde wanai." The words lightly left his breath as he walked into the room. Kame didn't tell the family what he saw or allow them to hear his whisper to the seishin. He didn't make any grand gestures. Instead, he simply waited. Kame didn't know how long it would take for the Shinigami to disappear, but if he had anything at this moment, it was time. So he waited.

And he waited. When his stomach growled loudly, the family asked him to sit at their table to eat a simple meal of soup, rice, pickles, and fish. And when his belly growl became a yawn, they slid open the door opposite the boy's room that had a clean shikubuton and kakebuton—a cotton comforter. Kame didn't fully understand why, but for the first time in a long time, he slept soundly.

In the morning, the boy took a deep breath. His lashes fluttered against cheeks rising with warmth and color.

"His fever broke!"

Screams of excitement could be heard throughout the home. But that wasn't what woke Kame. What jolted him awake was a hug from the boy's mother, who had spent days afraid she would lose her only son forever. It was the hug from the grandmother that brought him to his knees, to better suit the petite lady. Her heartbeat reminded Kame it had been a long time since anyone had hugged him.

The heaviness of the coins they placed in his palms felt new to him too. Counting them, he was surprised by the doctor's fee. After he had his last meal with the family, Kame slid on his getas and stepped out into the fresh morning air that he drew in with a deep breath. *So this is what it feels like to heal people? Is this what the Shinigami wanted me to know?*

"You, the one who healed Itaro! Can you heal my Yūkichi too?"

She had approached him as Kame was placing a rather large mouthful of soba noodles topped with the crispiest tempura in his mouth. He had decided to treat himself to one of the town's many busy food stalls where you ate standing up! Kame had never seen or tasted anything like it before. *This will make a glorious last meal before I meet my wife.*

But as his chopsticks were chasing around the last of the soba noodles and sweet eel, this woman came up and yelled at him. It wasn't so much of a harassing yell as a harassing plea. Kame wanted to be left alone. He wanted to have a full belly before he walked out to the bridge again. But this woman was pleading with him. Her husband was sick, and she wanted him to come and heal him just as she had healed the young boy. Kame wasn't sure if he could. By the sound of it, it seemed like her husband might be too severely ill.

"I will come and see what I can do," he sighed at last. Kindly, he warned the woman that there were limitations. He didn't exactly specify that it all rested on whether or not he saw a giant, knife-toothed-grinning, ghoul-like creature bending over her husband's feet. *Best to keep that detail to myself.*

The lattices of the house were fully shut. Kame squinted against the dim light that filtered through the tiny home. The woman explained that the light bothered her husband, so she had to keep it dark. When Kame slid off his getas, his stomach felt queasy against that familiar stench of sickness. Quickly, he asked to be shown to her husband's room.

The man convulsed erratically, flooding with sweat, then quickly curled into a shivering ball. There was something about the man's eyes, deep-set against high cheekbones lined from the stress of life, that reminded him of himself. They had to be around the same age. In this room, one man was healthy and a newly dubbed healer, but sad and lonely. The other man was groaning and disease-ridden as his wife looked on, praying for him.

Kame couldn't quite put into words the feelings that were rising.

When his eyes adjusted to the darkness, he saw the hulking outline of the Shinigami at the man's feet. His back was curved against the ceiling because he was so tall.

So I'll be able to save this man after all?

"I am not an Isha," Kame confessed to the woman, "so I don't know exactly what it is that he has. But am a healer and after seeing him, I do know this much—he won't die tonight. In fact, he will get better."

The woman nearly leapt with joy.

"Sōde wanai," Kame said.

"What did you say?"

"Sorry, nothing," Kame quickly replied, embarrassed that he had forgotten to whisper. "Just a useless saying I learned recently."

This time, his "useless saying" didn't result in him waiting very long. In a half an hour the Shinigami was gone, and the man was already looking a little better. Surprisingly, Kame felt satisfied seeing the woman's tears and screams turn to joy as she showered her husband with hugs and kisses. He even thought he overheard them say something about the stars.

When Kame finished, he used his healer's fee to book a room in a ryokan. Healing was tiring. What a rush of emotions he had felt these last few days. If he was honest with himself, the family of the young boy—feeling their arms around him—made all the sorrow that he had been carrying for the last few months disappear. But when he saw the woman stroking the cheek of her husband while they giggled together—that shoved that sorrow right back into his heart and stung even more.

Morning came and he slid into his getas. No more waiting to see his wife. He had put that off for far too long. Hadn't he obeyed the Shinigami's wishes? He had saved two people from death. Now wasn't he allowed to have a little relief and joy in his life? Walking out into the sunrise, he awkwardly realized that the day had a different purpose for him. There were people waiting who had heard of his story.

At first, Kame wanted to say no to their requests, but the Shinigami must have sensed this, because Kame swore he saw that menacing grin in the crowds. So Kame repeated what he did the day before. He let each person know he'd have to see their loved one to know if they could be saved. He whispered the secret words to the Shinigami sulking at the feet of the sick. Before long, he was known as the town's healer.

That name—Kame the healer—rippled like light throughout the large town. What Kame hadn't realized at first was that on the other side of the bridge, opposite the remote village where he had lived for most of his life, hundreds of thousands of people lived in a single town. So, in this town, there was always someone to heal. And Kame was always called.

One by one, their stories, hugs, tears, and smiles leaned into his heart until a ripple of change swept over him. Shockingly, he slowly lost the desire to walk out to the bridge with the single purpose of ending his life. Sometimes, on a particularly clear night, he would go to the bridge to look up at the stars, but only to sit and enjoy a sweet memory. "I still love you," he'd say to his wife.

After many years grayed his hair, he was thankful that time and a new purpose had numbed his sorrow. He could love the memory of the most beautiful woman he knew, while still being happy and busy in his new life across the bridge.

But one thing had been bothering him lately. Hadn't the Shinigami who had first greeted him all those years ago mentioned that a person could not be saved if a Shinigami was at their head? Kame had never seen this before—all his patients had a Shinigami at their feet. Must be a mistaken memory, Kame thought to himself.

The fact that the memory rippled and poked and bothered Kame should have been a sign to the old man. For it was a warning that would save his life.

One cold morning, an aristocrat called for Kame. A noblewoman from an elite household had just given birth, and the family feared an evil spirit was gambling for her life. Kame was thankful he didn't have other clients that morning—one thing he'd learned after spending more than a decade in the town was that the aristocrats weren't kind when they heard "no." So it wasn't long before Kame was standing in the noble's bedroom, surrounded by an army of her female attendants in white robes.

In the middle of the expansive room was a bed unlike anything Kame had seen before. Instead of a single shikubuton on the floor, this bed hovered a good two feet over the ground, supported by four stilts that rose high to the ceiling. The shikubuton rested between these four stilts and was double the usual size. Almost hidden in this massive bed sat the mistress of the house. Her forehead was so damp with sweat and she looked so pitiful that Kame instantly felt a strong desire to help her.

"What are you doing here?" Kame suddenly gasped.

"What's wrong?" A flurry of attendants surrounded Kame.

"Nothing," Kame said as she stared into the yellow eyes of the Shinigami sulking at the head of the bed. The seishin could stand erect in this large room, but instead it chose to bend over, grinning at Kame as it came close to his face.

The old man was terrified. "Tur-t-turn the bed around!" Kame shouted. "Quickly, we must turn the bed around!"

When the servants looked at him in confusion, he quickly explained. "This is too grave a sickness. The bed must be turned around so the lady's feet are facing south. That will drain the sickness from her body." Kame half believed what he was saying. It was the best way to chase away that old memory that had been bothering him.

A dozen female attendants gathered around their lady and made the bed face in the opposite direction. Kame patted the beads of sweat on his forehead with a handkerchief. It would be okay. The spirit didn't move as the bed was turned around. Now, it rested at the feet of the woman. Everything would be okay. He'd simply have to say the words, and the spirit would disappear.

Kame stood next to the woman. He was too terrified to look at the spirit. Those knife-like grins had always unsettled him.

"Sōde wanai," Kame finally said. But something didn't feel right and he closed his eyes, waiting. When he opened them, he screamed. "No! No! Shinigami, please!"

Flashing before Kame's eyes, he saw his candle. With one flick from the Shinigami, the flame burned out.

The way of medicine is solely through chu and sei.

As Kame lay on the floor dying, he finally understood what the saying meant. It was about truth. There was no way he could trick or lie to his patients. It would have been better to tell the aristocrat that his wife was dying than to lie. That was what the Shinigami had wanted him to learn all those years ago. That was why he had become a healer, bound by the truth about where a Shinigami was sitting and when a person's flame had burned out.

As the final light of life left his body, Kame felt thankful for the life he had led and glad his time had finally come to leave it all behind in the darkness.

There is a reason Shinigami keep their mouths of knife-like teeth open wide. The gaping shape isn't a grin, as Kame had always thought, but a warning. One should never try to trick, lie, or steal from a Shinigami. That's when you'll see the full expanse of that cavernous mouth— built to devour and chomp bodies and souls.

Because Kame had served and followed the Shinigami's words well all those years, only his body died that morning. His soul was allowed to live on and finally be reunited with a woman. Her name was Ai, and her spirit hadn't changed a day since she admired the human-like houses of her Sato-umi on the bridge.

THE LORD OF DEATH

In Southern Africa, there were several Indigenous nomadic tribes that spoke Khoe. Often referred to as Khoekhoe, these tribes traveled where the food went to hunt, gather, and forage for their provisions. Today, while they are recognized by organizations such as UNESCO, few of these clans still exist today.

As a group of peoples whose very existence was tied to the changes of the earth, their deities and myths are tightly bound to nature. These gods and goddesses are supreme beings that can give life and death, bring rain, or take away vital plants. In one myth, the personification of death is fully manifested when a god chooses to take the life of an entire village. But when one fights back to save his people, what will be his fate?

They say the sun was angry at the plains of Namibia that day. Mukuru— the sun goddess—smoldered the ground and eroded the once-moist soil until it was as brittle as the bones the vultures left behind. This wasn't the first time she battered all that was once fertile with her heated gaze. And those who built their tribe from the dust of bones and evaporating souls hoped it wouldn't be her last.

Gaunab was one of those—a god hailing from the expanse beyond the moon and shooting stars. The tip of his greenish-silver arrow grazed the topaz-hued fluff of clouds he hid behind. Running across the sky, he saw that a tribe of humans was dying out, one by one falling into the craters of the dry earth, ready to become souls that he would add to his own tribe—for he was the god of death.

What happens when a person dies is this: Gaunab readies his bow. They say black bones fused into the shape of a man to form the god, but his eyes are pure white—for they see the time when someone is close to death. Gaunab can almost feel the air leaving his own body, as if he is the one whose last breath has sucked his soul into a luminous flow of light up to the heavens. Then Gaunab shoots his arrow.

Our eyes never see Gaunab's arrow or the light of souls as they ascend. All we know is the silence when a soul leaves and a body becomes no more than the dust of the earth, weeping with slowly disappearing memories. As each new soul wanders into the skies, Gaunab absorbs their stories of coming and going and the emotions a god like him isn't allowed to feel—enthusiasm, lust, ambition, fear, motherly love, anxiety.

Each emotion Gaunab absorbed from the ascending souls was more dazzling and precious than the last. For him, the process of death was more a reckless collection of rare objects than a discerning and compassionate welcome to the afterlife. In his frenzy of acquisition, he neglected to calculate which emotions he should and shouldn't absorb. So when he felt particularly abuzz with vengeance and pride, his actions drifted from the wisdom of gods into a tidal wave of vanity, foolishness, and anger.

Where is he? Gaunab peered over the clouds at a small village nestled between the plains and mountains of Namibia. His bow wanted to pierce and strip only one man of his life that day. Sure, there would be others, but it was that lone, flickering breath he had a violent urge to end.

On a normal day, the morning would still be cool from dew, offering a refreshing mist on the skin before the villagers would begin their routines. A fire would rise into the air—a fragrant aroma of meats and maize cakes roasting. Herders rallied their flocks to the hills to graze on the thick tufts of grasses that rose a good three feet from the ground. A trolley of women trailed down to the river to gather water. Tsui Goab, a hunter, readied his bow as he walked into the bush with the gatherers. Then he would look up at the heavens to give his quick prayer of thanks to the gods.

But today was not a normal day.

The sun had just begun driving its vivid heat over the sunken plains. Even before he saw the light, Tsui Goab felt the heat howl through his small hut of mud bricks and straw. For a second, he thought he recognized the heat as a fire, but then he realized there were no flames. So he rose and sat in the entrance of his hut finding a little respite from the baking sun.

What else could he do today? The sun had made it too hot to hunt, too hot to gather food, and worst of all, too hot to find water. Life on the Namibia plains was dying from the sun's livid flashes of anger. So all he felt he could do was sit and wait for death.

Gaunab felt glee rise through his chest when he saw the hunter. This emotion had been borrowed from the dead souls, too, and felt so different from the diplomatic stoicism that the gods were meant to feel. A song lifted into his lungs as he readied his arrow in his bow. The hunter reminded him much of himself. He admired his robust stature and his role as a leader and provider amongst his people. But it didn't matter—pridefully, Gaunab knew he was the better hunter, and today was the day he'd make the mighty Tsui Goab fall.

Because what Tsui Goab failed to do on normal days, when he sent his prayer of thanks to the gods, was to thank Gaunab. It didn't matter that Gaunab wasn't known to be particularly helpful, compassionate, or loving. Every being on Earth lavishly spilled out all manner of thanks for the earth, for life and death, vowing to show their reverence and thanks. So why not Tsui Goab?

How could the hunter leave out the name of the god of death? How could he not give thanks that his life was spared or that he was provided with game to feed his people? Foolish hunter, you will be the first of your villagers I will take today.

Today will be a day of reckoning. Mourning will be heard for miles from the herders who see the bones of their cattle poking out of their dead flesh. The people themselves are close to the gates of death.

Because the sun was angry, it had been many moons since the rains had fallen. The ground was hard and dry. There were no plants for the women to pick berries and nuts from. No water was found for their herd or for the villagers to moisten their own lips. Even the wildlife that would nourish their bellies during the dry season had migrated too far for the hunters to follow. The people were starving. They were dying. And the god of death was waiting.

He waited. And waited. Then, Gaunab started to pace. He scanned the village down below once again. Gaunab's patience had worn out. Why can't I shoot my arrow? Every black bone in his body told him that the hunter's time was soon, but almost mechanically, he knew that soon was not now. Exasperated, Gaunab decided *it's because I am in the sky. I am too far. I must go down and be closer—then I will feel that it is Tsui Goab's time to die.*

But a god doesn't simply walk into the world of humans and expect to blend in. He must transform—condense and adjust his form so everything about his image embodies the petite, two-armed, two-legged image of man and woman. Gaunab's godly form wasn't too far from the shape of man, but his onyx-hued skin lavishly stretched over muscles that would have made him a giant amongst men, and his white eyes shone like moons. He would have been too alarming. So as he descended, shaking the clouds with thunder, he chose to transform his eyes to a warm mocha hue and shrink to the size of Tsui Goab. Clad in a loincloth with a bow and arrow slung across his back, his feet touched the parched ground. He looked like a mortal now—one whose eyes gleamed with inhuman violence.

When they heard the thunder, the villagers poked out of their huts and turned to the heavens. They were so thirsty for the sound of rain that many of them mumbled prayers and lifted their hands. But the rumbling in the clouds did not return. And all they saw past the haze of heat that made the horizon shimmer was a tall man. No one knew who he was. With life now such a fragile thing, no one cared about the stranger's presence—except Tsui Goab, that is.

"Stranger, why have you come here?" Tsui Goab called out to the newcomer as he shielded his eyes from the sun. On a normal day he would have welcomed the stranger with water or mahangu soup—a stew of goat meat and rice. But today was not a normal day.

Rising to his feet drew a heavy breath from Tsui Goab. He could feel his muscles yearning for fuel, and each step toward the stranger wearied him. The night before, he had walked the surrounding land, listening for water, readying his bow for any animals that might be nearby. But when the first light of dawn settled over the horizon, his head hung heavy as he began the long walk back to his village—arms empty, bow unused. And if he was being honest with himself, this walk of defeat had been thus for many moons.

At least I can save this stranger. "Stranger, do you not see the state of my people? This land is barren. The rain has not come for many moon cycles. One would think that the sun is angry with us. But since I cannot save my people, I will try to save you. Gather what energy you have and find fertile lands to feed yourself and your tribe."

Tsui Goab's bare feet dragged up pools of dust as he walked. Gaunab could see how little strength the hunter had left. *Surely, the hunter's time is now.* His fingers restlessly fondled his bow. He looked to the heavens. His eyes swept back down over the village. *How many lives will I take tonight?* The thought drew a smile over his lips. But then it quickly faded.

Tsui Goab was standing in front of him now—too close. The hunter lifted one eye as he scanned the stranger.

"What did you say your name was?" the hunter asked.

"You may call me Khoe." Gaunab's words were calm, but his eyes challenged Tsui Goab.

"Khoe, where did you say you were from?"

"Farther than you have been, I'm sure."

Tsui Goab observed Gaunab's bow—a sliver of wood curled around a tightly wound piece of golden string.

"I have never seen any weapon like this before. So sleek. So strong. The craftsmanship is worthy of a god." Tsui Goab's eyes met Gaunab's glare.

Impudent hunter. How dare he challenge my disguise? He slid the arrow into the bow. You, Tsui Goab, will be the first to die, and everyone in your village will follow.

Seeing the bow readied, Tsui Goab took a step between the stranger and his village.

"God of death," he said, dropping to one knee. "Only a god could wield such a powerful bow and arrow. I know that my starving village is close to death." Tsui Goab looked up at the god. "The rains have dried up. This land has become barren. But we do not wish to die. So I ask that before you wield your arrow to take our lives, please hear my request."

A frown slid over Gaunab's face. Only one arrow was needed to cut through the air and pierce the flesh of every human in this village. Then their souls would all be his.

"Great god, your reputation precedes you," Tsui Goab continued.

What kind of god would I be if I did not hear this poor mortal's dying request? I am both mighty and merciful.

"God of death, your strength is known throughout the lands. They say you are mightier than the wild boar and more indomitable than ten gorillas." Tsui Goab spoke slowly. He wasn't entirely sure what to say. He knew that his people needed rain. And here, standing before him, was a god—a fearsome god who brought death and thunder.

How can I plead before him to save my people? How can I persuade this god to put down his weapon? Slowly, an idea formed in Tsui Goab's mind.

"In your godlike form, I could never hope to compete with you. But still, it would be my honor if I could challenge you to a fight. I am well respected amongst my people for my prowess and strength, so it would not be a dishonor to you. If I win, I ask that you bring the rains that would save my people. And if I lose, I offer you my life and the lives of all those in my village to be souls under your dominion."

Stupid, stupid boy. Tsui Goab was a rock of a man and in the past would have been an admirable foe to destroy in his human form. But the Tsui Goab standing before him today was sunken with protruding bones. Gaunab knew that he struggled to find strength to stand and was losing vigor with each flicker of his eyelids.

How can you even think you'd defeat a god? This fight will be over in seconds. Yet I am merciful. In moments like these—when mankind makes an unstable show of desperation—it is noble for me to throw them a bone, as they say.

Gaunab nodded in agreement.

The two men would fight. The rules were laid bare. No weapons. No powers. Each would fight as a mortal with his bare hands. A six-foot ring was dug into the red earth. Once the men entered, neither could leave. Whoever was pushed outside the drawn lines, or whoever caved and asked for mercy, would lose and declare the other the victor.

Upon hearing that Tsui Goab was going to fight the god of death to try to get them water, the villagers left their huts and gave the hunter what little provisions they had—water, bitter herbs, and bark. At first, Tsui Goab refused to take what the villagers offered. But swinging from one face to another, he saw in their eyes something he hadn't been able to give them during his many moonlit walks searching for food. *I've summoned the last centimeter of hope these people have.*

He took a long sip of hard-saved water and dug his teeth into the herbs and bark. The light meal wouldn't instantly bring back his robust frame, but it was enough to summon his final ounce of strength. *My people are telling me to win for them… for us.*

Under Mukuru's scorching fury, Tsui Goab and Gaunab stepped into the ring. With a shout from a village elder, the fight began.

How does one fight when they have nothing left to lose? One emotion Gaunab had never absorbed from the souls that ascended into the sky was desperation. But as his flesh struck Tsui Goab's and the two grappled and tumbled in the dust of the hard earth—he felt it. He couldn't quite call out the feeling by name, but he knew Tsui Goab was strengthened by the desire to save his people. And it seemed to expel all weakness from his body.

This human, even when weakened by hunger, is stronger than I thought he would be.

Gaunab was even surprised by a new physical emotion that hit him— pain. He noticed that his skin was battered at the edges from crashing into rocks and was peeling off in certain areas, exposing a flash of soft pink underflesh that swelled with blood. And while it wasn't entirely pleasant, the jagged stab of pain was new and exciting.

It went on like this for two days and two nights. Neither man tired nor gave in. Neither let his foot leave the ring drawn into the earth. Physically, they resembled each other—dark brown skin built around raw muscles. And even though only one of them was finely chiseled from the labor of hunting under the sun, both had an amphitheater of strength that fueled them. Gaunab puffed out his chest with the erratic excitement of attempting to beat his enemy. With deft skill, Tsui Goab adjusted his stance and tackles to steadily reserve his strength while observing how close his opponent's foot came to the edge of their drawn circle.

The anger of the sun transformed into the wailing softness of the moon. If the night air offered relief, it was very little. Throughout the night their skin glistened with pearls of sweat as the two men frantically clashed into one another again and again. From dusk to dusk their fight continued. Then, when Mukuru rose on the third day, a shout was heard.

"The fight is over! A victor has been made!" The village elder raised his staff. Just as the two men had stayed awake fighting night and day, so too had the old man, folding himself into a chair outside of the ring to keep a watchful eye on whose foot would leave first.

At the sound of the cry, every villager who had the strength scattered around the circle. Standing inside, heaving from the climb to victory, was Tsui Goab. Thrown outside, lying on his back, was Gaunab, seized by the awareness of defeat. Murmurs rippled through the crowd. Although it was what they had clapped their hands in front of their breasts and prayed for, few could believe it. But there it was before their eyes. Tsui Goab was their victor.

"Tsui Goab!" A god should have accepted defeat with pious composure. But Gaunab had foolishly absorbed rage. So now he ferociously charged at the hunter. The speed at which he moved wasn't human. No, he didn't care to reserve his strength to match that of the villagers around him anymore. He was a god, and he reanimated himself with all of his strength to grab a rock larger than his own mortal body and fling it at the hunter's knees.

Tsui Goab fell to the ground, clenching his teeth in agonizing pain. His blood moistened the parched earth as he clawed at the ground, but he couldn't rise. He was already in Gaunab's grip.

"Today you won, hunter. I will honor my word. Your tribe will receive rain. But for your insolence to challenge a god, I have broken your knees. You will never walk again as a mortal. Remember this day. Remember whom you kneel before." Gaunab shoved Tsui Goab's face into the ground. On his knees, the hunter heard the clouds shudder and rumble.

What good are legs if your village is dying? If this is the sacrifice I must make to save my people, then I gladly accept this fate. The pain felt like it was burrowing deep into Tsui Goab's mind. Even his acceptance couldn't extinguish it. He gnashed his teeth, holding in the waves of pain. "Help," he sang out. Like a song—garbled with his tears—he called out to his people.

And they gladly answered. The breath of hope Tsui Goab had given them gave lightness to their feet and strength to their arms as they gathered around the hunter and lifted him. Even without the nourishment of the rain, they felt more alive now. The walk to the hunter's hut seemed like a light-hearted skip. They placed him down on his mat to rest, tending to his broken legs with soft wrappings of dried grass. Even Mukuru's anger was dissipating—the sun cooled into a soft breeze, offering relief to the worn village. Because of Tsui Goab, they would now have rain. And even though it hadn't come yet, they were thankful. Looking to the sky, someone began to sing. A song flowed from their lips praising the young hunter and his bravery.

From the heavens, the music magnetized Gaunab's anger. *How could a mere mortal defeat me? How could the villagers sing to this mortal, but forget to give thanks to me?*

Waves of thunder shuddered the blackening sky. But Gaunab's tantrums couldn't bring rain any more than a toddler's pounding fists and wails could. He was the god of death whose arrows were the precursor to souls ascending to the afterlife. No matter how violently he crashed the turquoise-hued clouds into a vacuum of black rage, he could not bring rain. That was something he'd have to ask the other gods for. And that would involve relaying the story of his defeat and pleading with them to help him fulfill his word. For a second he resented the idea so much that he considered walking away from his word, but just as his arrows could not take a man before his time had come, he couldn't walk away from his word. So down came a shower of embarrassment for Gaunab.

The god of death should have known that the other gods already knew of his defeat. After all, how could Mukuru miss anything under the watchful light of the sun? Peeling back the clouds of the heavens, the gods looked down at the mortal who had challenged the god of death. They watched the man and the god grapple in the hard earth. They heard Gaunab give his final words and blows of anger when he broke Tsui Goab's knees. Whispering amongst themselves, they made sneering remarks about Gaunab's outbursts of anger and praised the hunter for his sacrifice. *The hunter has the courage, compassion, honor, trustworthiness, strength, and discernment of a god.*

When Tsui Goab's eyes flickered into a deep sleep, the goddess Mukuru visited him in his dreams. They say that the goddess has no shape or form, that she is only a beam of pure light that cradles you in feelings of love.

"Brave hunter," she called to him. "I see your pain. I have seen your acts of bravery, how you risked your life to save the lives of your people."

Once the goddess spoke, Tsui Goab felt a wave of serenity illuminate his very being. His body felt lifted from the struggle of pain that vibrated from his legs. And the parched dryness of his throat was gone. He was at peace.

"You have proven your strength against Gaunab, showing that you are his equal. But the god that you fought does not have the power to honor your agreement. So, young hunter, I am giving the gift to you. From this day on, your name will be Tsui Goab no more. They will call you *Gamab*—the benevolent god of life and rain. Your wounds are deadly, but don't be afraid. When you die, you will be reborn and will have these gifts that will save your people."

Mukuru's light faded from the small hut, leaving Tsui Goab writhing with pain again in the darkness. But before long he fell into a peaceful sleep again, the deepest sleep the hunter had ever had.

Dawn found the hunter's body cold and empty. His soul had ascended. And when the villagers found him, their ripples of mourning grew louder and louder, a tsunami of wails heard for miles. When his body was carefully cleaned and wrapped, their cries advanced into chants and songs that lasted two days. This was the burial ceremony.

It should come as no surprise that Gaunab was still too full of pride to ask the other gods for rain. Instead, his being vibrated with delight as the hunter's death advanced closer and closer to its fated time. And when that time came, he swiftly shot his arrow into Tsui Goab's chest. But like many of Gaunab's plans that foolishly disregarded honor and the very people he was meant to welcome into the afterlife, this plan failed.

Where is he? For days the god of death waited for the hunter to enter the realm of the dead. But wherever he looked in the sky, the hunter was nowhere to be found.

"You won't find the hunter here," Mukuru said. The presence of the supreme being startled the god of death. "I know what you have done, Gaunab. From the corners of the heavens, I watched as the hunter challenged you. I observed your jealousy and witnessed you delivering a mortal blow when you should have kept your word. Your actions are rooted in anger and show the true colors of the emotions that you have absorbed.

"Your lack of discernment and your greed have demonstrated that you are not worthy of the gift of life and death, so you will share this responsibility with the one who has defeated you. He has proved he is your equal." With no more to say, Mukuru left swiftly.

Gaunab peered over the clouds to view the land of the humans. He could hear that the villagers were surprised by something. He heard shouting and yelps of joy.

There was shuffling within the coverings draped over the dead body. The body was moving, slowly taking off the fabric that covered his face. Tsui Goab was alive again! But when the villagers called out his name, he told them he was no longer Tsui Goab.

"A goddess came to me in my sleep," Tsui Goab began. "She told me that I would die, but I would live again. I would no longer be mortal—I would become the god who would give my people rain."

He walked outside the hut to the dry ground. Raising his hands to the sky, he felt a new power surge through his veins. He could feel the clouds swell with water, and that water poured down onto the cracked ground beneath his feet. "From now on, my name shall be Gamab, the god of life-giving rain!"

That morning, Mukuru no longer aimed her scorching anger at the ground of mankind. That day, a procession of all that was needed to survive blossomed from the once-hardened earth. At the same time the rains fell from the heavens, so too did Mukuru shine, and the two gods mingled their powers into a flow of colors. From purple to yellow, each color was present in this feat of beauty that arched across the sky and swept down into the horizon. Some say it was a promise that her anger would never dry out the lands again. Others tell the tale of how she created those beautiful colors in the sky as a welcome gift for the new god, Gamab.

On the last day of the summer showers, Gamab's body and soul left his people. He would no longer live his days as a human, hunting to provide for his village. Instead, when it was time, his form ascended and twisted into an entirely new being—like a human, but larger, and gleaming like black enamel. Behind tufts of pastel clouds, he sat next to another god he had met once—Gaunab. Gaunab's poor judgment in collecting emotions and neglecting his duties as the god of death had forced him to share his title.

Now they say there are two gods of death—Gaunab, whose arrows of death take away the lives of those who have lived wicked lives on this earth, and Gamab, who is benevolent and gives rain that waters the plants and nourishes his people.

THE GODDESS OF THE SEA

In Greenland, when an Inuk—a subculture of the Indigenous peoples often referred to as Inuit—dies, their bodies are wrapped in caribou skin and their feet are pointed south. Some say this is to honor the goddess of the sea, Sedna, who welcomes all spirits to Adlivun. After three days the spirit is taken into the depths of the ocean. For it is here that Sedna, the mother of the sea, resides.

Little is known about Adlivun in Western culture. But one story remains—the origin story of the goddess. Sedna is also known as Arnakuagsak or Arnaqquassaaq. Traditionally, the Inuits imbued nature with spirits and personalities that could either give or take away life. As the spirit at the bottom of the ocean, Sedna can provide the Inuits with bounty or withhold the means to survive.

In every town, there's a woman. Men turn their heads when she walks by. Mothers whisper their praises as she passes. Even children smile and admire her when she kneels down to pat them on the head. And many are green with envy, knowing they can never quite aspire to her beauty or receive the admiration that so easily comes to her.

In the Arctic, on an island just east of Baffin Bay where the icebergs are dense and mountains shelter the people from easterly winds, stands a village. In this village lived a woman named Sedna. She was that woman.

Sedna was beautiful. Waves of thick black hair joyously framed her caramel skin and ruby lips, invitingly parting to a wide smile. She was witty too. Wise words and clever jokes were always leaving her lips, garnering her esteem from villagers. Her hands were skilled as well—her craftsmanship saw her family dressed in the finest clothes.

Using the skins from her father's hunts, she made sumptuous cloaks lined in fur and embroidered with dancing whales, seals, and other life of the sea. Kneeling by the fire with her mother, Sedna charred and fermented the meats her father hunted. He provided their family with plenty of fatty meats to warm their bellies or barter with to gain the luxuries that lined their warm home.

For Sedna, life was perfect. Sadly, perfect never lasts long.

It was during the migration of the cod and halibut that Sedna began to feel that life would not be so perfect anymore. As the fish began to flood the bay, bringing a bounty of flavorful new meats into her home, Sedna noticed a new flood of life within her own body.

"You are a woman now," her mother said to her.

"You are able to be married now," her father told her.

Soon, change migrated into Sedna's life. The men whose heads once turned when she walked by began to turn up in her home, accompanying her father after his hunt. Likewise, the mothers would join Sedna and her mother over the fire as they dried and seasoned the meats.

"I have a son," they would always say as their fingers examined the fine threads of Sedna's embroidery. Or they'd speak of a so-and-so who had a son, a cousin, a brother, or an adopted son who was skilled as a hunter and always caught succulent meats with his traps.

Sedna silently sat through many meals ruined by the company of the men from her village. Their stares and hungry smiles unsettled her. Their awkward jokes or bragging words about their successful hunts soured the meats in her mouth.

Each man upset Sedna. So each fisherman, hunter, or son of so-and-so was sent home, unsuccessful at wooing the prize woman of their village.

The winter winds came and went. The spring migration of birds and fish ebbed and flowed. Soon, Sedna was older, growing ever more beautiful and more skilled, her happiness and ease evident in her full cheeks and round curves.

She remained the desire of the men from her village and soon, as word spread of her beauty and fine age to become a wife, she also became the desire of men from afar. But with each man who came and left, she also became the despair of her father. For soon, the gracious admiration from the elderly women of their village turned to hushed words of disapproval.

"There he goes, the man with the daughter who thinks she is too good to marry one of our men," they'd say as he passed.

"Poor old man. He does not know that Sedna's beauty will fade, and he'll soon have an old maid he'll have to hunt for," another would chuckle.

At last, her father's anger boiled over.

"Wicked daughter! How could you bring such shame onto this family?" he yelled. "If you wish to eat, then you must marry. Your old mother and I will care for you no more!"

Still, Sedna persisted in her disobedience and refusal to adhere to tradition. Even though her father's words sparked fear in her belly, she stood strong in her decision not to marry any of the men who turned her stomach when they sat to dine in her home.

Then one day, something changed. The current brought warm waters to the southern tip of the bay. Sea eagles and geese flew in abundance over the clear waters. It was during this season that a new visitor was welcomed into Sedna's home.

The man sitting at the table of fine meats and berries prepared for their meal was a stranger to Sedna. In fact, no one from her village knew who he was. He was tall and handsome, with a strong nose and wide arms that held the promise that he was a voracious hunter. His fine clothes also suggested his skill at hunting in the Arctic.

Like most men her father welcomed into their hut, the stranger spoke of meats he caught. His eyes glowed with stories of his bounty— buttery cod and extravagantly large halibut.

But this time, Sedna did not feel he was bragging. She believed him.

The handsome stranger wooed her with promises that he would be able to provide her with plenty of food to eat and furs and blankets to keep her warm in the Arctic winds. And when he stood to leave and asked for Sedna's hand in marriage, she didn't say no. For several days, a sweet smile formed across her chestnut cheeks as she replayed his words. For several days and nights, Sedna thought only of him. As if under a spell, she brought the news to her father and mother. Sedna had finally said yes.

News of Sedna's marriage spread quickly throughout the village. Curious about the stranger their prized Sedna had said yes to, the villagers excitedly whispered amongst themselves.

"How curious it is that no one knows this stranger," one villager exclaimed. "It is foolish to be blinded by good looks and wealth," another warned. "Who can say they know his parents or can speak of the good morals he was raised with?" "She will have the choicest meats to eat and furs to wear!" "How lucky are her mother and father to know their daughter will be well taken care of."

Soon, Sedna said good-bye to the villagers and the bay that had been her home for eighteen years. With her few belongings, she huddled in a boat with her husband and set sail to his island. Throughout the journey across the choppy seas, Sedna was wide-eyed with excitement thinking about the luxuries that awaited her. She admired the intricate stitches of her husband's fine furs, so beautiful, unlike anything she had seen before. She dreamt of the luscious meats that he had spoken of.

But as quickly as Sedna's smile had come, so too did it fade.

As a young child, the old men and women of Baffin Island spoke of the terrible spirits of the air and sea they must be careful not to upset. Angakoks—men and women gifted with magic to appease the spirits—lifted their hands to the sky, begging for mercy. They told fishermen to cast organ meats into the sea as sacrifices.

"Most of all, beware that you do not anger the Kokksaut," the old Angakoks would say. "He is the raven of the gray sky who looks down on us from his cliff, summoning terrible storms when he is angry."

As her husband tied and steadied the boat on the rocky shore, Sedna realized she could see no huts or boats of other fishermen from the village. No smoke rose from the bright fires of men and women smoking delicate meats and staying warm. Instead, everything around her was gray—from the ground covered in stones to the sky and the rocky cliffs in the distance.

"What is this place?" Sedna questioned her husband. "Where are the villagers? Where is your hut?"

No words left her husband's lips. Silently he led her up a steep hill, her questions and protests left unanswered. At last they stopped. The stranger turned to face his wife. What Sedna saw next caused her to scream.

Against the bleak sky at the top of the gray cliff was a large nest. Her husband stood in front of the nest and as gusts of wind whipped around them, his face began to change. The strong nose stretched out, becoming wider and sharper than a sword. His shoulders expanded into a fluster of black feathers. Within seconds, the handsome stranger transformed into a giant raven.

"Kokksaut!" Sedna shrieked in horror as the spirit towered over her.

"My bride," Kokksaut responded. "I have watched you over these last few years, flying above your village. Even from the sky, your beauty outshines all. And no man can match your wit and skill." He expanded his wings over the giant nest. "Such a prize you are, I vowed to make you mine!"

Fear shook the words that came out of Sedna's mouth. "But you are a spirit. Not a man. My father gave me to a man who would keep me warm with fine meats and furs," she cried in protest. "You lied."

"I warn you, do not anger me." The spirit's eyes narrowed. "I spoke only of the halibut and cod. I told you my home was large," he said, walking toward the edge of the cliff. "You will eat good meats, but your food will be raw, as there is no fire allowed here. You will live in this large nest. On top of this cliff you must stay, and you will make me happy."

At these words, the giant raven flew off into the gray clouds that swam over Sedna's head.

A sadness that Sedna had never known before swept over her. Sometimes, fury swept over her too. Each day, Kokksaut would fly over the sea and return to the cliff bringing Sedna raw fish to eat. Each night wild winds caused her to shiver in her sleep.

Soon those shivers turned into weeping, a sorrowful song that the winds blew over the sea and into the quiet bay where her father lived. It had been two months since his daughter was wed. He hadn't seen her, and while he knew he should be joyful that she was now married to such a handsome and fine hunter, an aching pain filled him every evening when he thought of her. Each night he awoke thinking that the winds outside his hut sounded like his daughter crying.

Finally, Sedna's father paddled out to sea in his canoe. As he drew closer to the island where his daughter now lived, the sorrowful song of the sea became clearer and clearer. Now he knew what the song was.

"Sedna!" he yelled when he reached the island. No voice answered him save the mournful melody floating down from a cliff. Sedna's father climbed the cliff and when he reached the top, tears filled his eyes.

Huddled in a corner of a giant nest was his Sedna. Her body was no longer wrapped in fine furs and skins; her coat was tattered from the harsh conditions. Her caramel skin was scratched from the rough branches of the nest. The alluring luster in her eyes had left.

"My daughter, what has happened?"

"Kokksaut. The stranger was merely disguised as a human to trick me into marrying him," his daughter weakly replied.

With much pain in his heart, the old man swept his daughter into his arms. She was lighter than when she had left his home. He carried her down the cliff and placed her in his canoe. It was a terrible thing that had happened to his daughter, and though he feared inciting Kokksaut's anger against his family, his heart was broken at the thought of leaving Sedna in this place.

So with a push, the old man sailed his canoe out to sea, beginning his journey home. For a while all was silent on the water. But then the old man heard a terrifying scream. It was coming from the cliff. Kokksaut had returned to his nest with his daily bounty of fish to find that his bride was no longer there.

Scanning the island and surrounding waters, Kokksaut soon saw the old man's small boat. There, sitting next to the old man, was his bride. When the spirit realized what had taken place in his absence, his anger darkened the sky above them. He flapped his wings with such ferocity that a storm tore apart the seas. The canoe violently rocked back and forth as the waves thrashed. With each knock, the old man thought he would die. He lost control and almost flipped over, throwing Sedna out into the sea. Swimming back to the boat, Sedna clung to its side.

"Father, help me!" Sedna screamed above the deadly storm. "I cannot pull myself up. Please pull me up before I drown."

The old man was afraid. He thought of his wife and younger children waiting for him to return. Who would brave the Arctic winds to hunt for them if he died at sea?

"I must not anger the raven spirit any more," he whispered to himself. "Sedna!" he screamed against the storm. "Let go!"

Shocked, Sedna refused. Her nails clawed tighter into the boat, causing it to tilt dangerously.

"Let go!" Again her father called out. But she would not. "Selfish child!"

Realizing that he would die if she did not let go, the old man pulled out his ulu knife. In desperation he brought the blade down on the fingers of his first child.

Sedna's scream was the last sound he heard from his child. He watched as her face sank to the bottom of the sea. Despite his cruel action, the old man cried for his daughter. But the winds stopped and the waves settled, allowing him to make his way home. So he felt what he had done was right.

Below his boat, dragged down by the weight of her clothes, was Sedna. Her hands pulsated from the pain. Her heart felt betrayed.

The Angakoks used to say that the spirits would help those who had been wronged if their hearts were truly pure. As Sedna sank to the underworld, she prayed to the gods. In the depths of the sea, she asked the spirits to make her torment stop.

Her heart must have been pure, for suddenly the pain was gone. And somehow, despite being sure that she would die, Sedna felt the blood running through her veins. Soon, she realized too that she could breathe underwater.

Miraculously, she watched as her body transformed in the depths of the underworld. Her fingers, severed by the blade of her father, turned into an array of sea creatures—fish, walruses, whales. At the bottom of the ocean, Sedna became a powerful spirit. It was now she who controlled the creatures of the sea that the hunters relied on for their livelihood.

The Angakoks could feel her spirit. When Sedna's father returned to Baffin Bay, they shook their staffs at the old man.

"It is a terrible thing that you have done. The spirits help only those who have been wronged, and now the spirit of the one that you have wronged is powerful enough to take revenge on us."

And Sedna did have her revenge. She knew how to hide the sea creatures from the hunters and how to make them plentiful. When she angrily remembered her father's cruelty, no fish came into the nets of the men seeking food for their families.

The Angakoks were called on by the hunters to appease the goddess. Using their magic, they swam to the depths of the underworld to find Sedna. With no fingers to use as a comb, Sedna's long hair was tangled and painful. The Angakoks combed her thick hair, gently smoothing out both the snarls and her anger with their repetitive motions. When her hair was sleek once more, the seas swelled with life. The hunters and the fisherman could be successful again. But now they knew better than to ignore the goddess in the deep. After each successful hunt, the hunters sacrificed the organs to Sedna, allowing them to sink to the bottom of the sea.

Long after Sedna's family died, the villagers kept this tradition, always being careful to share the tale of the woman more beautiful than all others and how her sorrow controlled the sea. Even now, the children sing songs about her.

> That woman down there beneath the sea,
> That woman down there beneath the sea,
> She wants to hide the seals from us.
> These hunters in the dance house,
> They cannot mend matters.
> They cannot mend matters.
> Into the spirit world
> Will go I,
> Where no humans dwell.
> Set matters right will I.
> Set matters right will I.[9]

---

9 James Houston, "The Goddess of the Sea: The Story of Sedna," *Canadian Encyclopedia*, last edited April 23, 2015.

CAMP OF GHOSTS

Long, long ago, before the sun, before our father or grandmothers were born or the white people knew anything about the rose-colored mountains lined black with pine trees, a sandy slope of land called the Sand Hills was created. Hidden in shadows by the rose-colored mountains, the Sand Hills were for those whose time had come to an end on this earth but whose spirits lived on. Much like the world of the living, the Sand Hills had a sky and mountains and trees and rivers. But unlike our world, it was cast in a deep shade that blocked the sun and shrouded everything in fog. Such was the resting place of the dead.

Now, many avoided the Sand Hills. For it was said that many living souls were lost wandering there.

As centuries passed and mankind lived and died, it became known that the voices of loved ones who recently passed could still be heard by those they left behind.

"Come with me," they'd say. "Let's live our days together forever," another voice would echo. "All you have to do is cross the line into the shadows of the rose-colored mountains."

And if the living were not careful, they were mesmerized and persuaded by their lost loved ones to wander into the Sand Hills, where their souls would be forever torn from the living.

"Do you love me?" Kitchi smiled at his wife.

His wide cheekbones stood atop strong shoulders. The shiny, thick plaits that fell to his waist mimicked his thick muscles. Many women blushed at the twinkle in his dark eyes when he set out with his bow and arrow. His brown skin—darkened by hours spent on the hot plain—glistened during the warm summer months, they said. But for all the admiring gazes, Kitchi only ever noticed one.

The sun was setting behind the mountains. Kitchi wasn't looking for an answer. He knew what his wife would say next. Each night, before the first star twinkled in the dark sky, Kitchi would playfully nudge his wife.

"Of course I do," she always replied.

Her name was Nuttah, and she was the daughter of a medicine man. She had a moon-shaped face with rosy cheeks that made her look years younger. But it was her almond eyes shining with wisdom and a quick wit that quickly caught his heart. Soon, Kitchi's strong spirit and laughter won Nuttah's heart.

"How much?" he'd say.

The sky was darkening quickly. Soon more stars came, until the twinkling patterns were more numerous than grains of sand. *Has anyone ever tried to count them all?*

"Do you see that star there and there? And there? And there? Count them all, my love, and that number wouldn't even begin to be close to how much I love you."

How was it that after all these nights, his wife could still offer a clever saying? He followed her gaze higher and higher as she playfully whispered in his ear. Last night she had said that her love was all-encompassing, like the buffalo whose meat and fat provided rich meals to feed their family and whose hides were cured for blankets, robes, and teepee covers.

Did she take pleasure in finding answers for him, or did she tolerate his question out of love? Whether she enjoyed these games, he would never know.

The fire quietly died in their teepee as they fell asleep. Kitchi tightly held Nuttah in his arms until the first signs of morning lifted his eyelids. Softly he kissed her warm cheek before leaving their home. Today, like every day since he had chosen a life as a hunter, he gathered his bow, arrow, and spear. He mounted his horse and rode onto the wide plains, carefully studying the short grass for signs that the buffalo had treaded through. He turned over leaves of bushes to reveal succulent blackberries he could take home.

He was never alone on these journeys. Riding by his side on her chestnut-colored horse was Pi'tamaka. Her tightly woven braids beat in rhythm with the horse's gait as the fringe of her long suede dress flapped in the wind. *There will probably be songs written about those beating braids, Kitchi thought.*

The two met when they were children and the camp was gathered together to create the piskun, or trap, for the bison. She had scolded him and swatted away his tiny fingers for tying the rope wrong. Full of shame, Kitchi fought back the urge to cry, but there was something about Pi'tamaka's eyes, even with her brow furrowed, that was kind and reassuring. Everyone said that she was like this. It was why everyone agreed she should be the leader of his camp's hunting expeditions. She was the only one in their camp given this honor. Proudly, he watched as a shaman entrusted her with the bison rock, a talisman that had great power in calling the animals.

Kitchi laughed to himself. One might think she was riding with him when they rode side by side like this, but in reality, it was her beating braids that he and the other hunters followed. Her bow was strong and steady. Kitchi couldn't ask for a better hunter to lead him or a better companion to help him bring back choice meats to his wife.

The sky was red when Kitchi returned home. As he dismounted his horse, he wondered what clever saying Nuttah would have for him. But when he entered his teepee, an unsettling feeling told him that this night would be different.

The first star shone brightly in the sky. And then another. Kitchi didn't ask if she loved him. Soon the entire sky was ablaze with stars, but their teepee remained silent. Nuttah lay there all night long staring into the dark. A blade-like pain in her chest continuously nudged her awake. Soon it threatened her lungs, making each breath a labored wheeze where she felt like she couldn't get enough air. At dawn her eyelids were still cracked open, tired from the labor of the night, but too afraid to close. What if the next tight breath didn't come? But she couldn't explain this to Kitchi. All she could do was moan. And all Kitchi could do was kneel by his wife's side.

On the mornings when the hunting party went out onto the plain, Pi'tamaka and Kitchi met at the border of their camp. They were the first two to go out, to scout and call the buffalo that the hunters would then sacrifice and kill. Pi'tamaka had never worried that she wouldn't see the easygoing smile she had known for the past five years that they hunted together. But today when he didn't arrive, she felt an unsettling twist in her stomach. She turned her horse around and rode toward the teepee that Kitchi shared with his wife. With the sun at her back, she stood in the doorframe of the dark teepee.

"I cannot go with you today," Kitchi said in a tone sharper than he had intended.

The first time Pi'tamaka rode out onto the plains with Kitchi, all he could talk about was his wife. She was there in the beauty of the flowers whose blossoms would soon turn into berries. She was as warm as the sun that cradled his face along the plains. Apparently, his arms were even made stronger by her. It seemed to Pi'tamaka that he had never intended to express this all to her—it almost slipped out. But every day she had known him, it was clear how his wife's very existence was tied to his own.

As Pi'tamaka looked at the sunlight on Nuttah's moon-shaped face, the sharp twisting in her stomach only worsened. The berry hue that usually colored Nuttah's lips and cheeks was gone.

"I will call Ni-namp'-skan."

These were the only words Pi'tamaka could offer. It seemed foolish to ask what was wrong when she already knew. It would have been odd if she entered the teepee and offered a meaningless hug. No, the best thing she could do now was to go and get the one man who could help her friend's wife.

A warm breeze cradled her face as she turned away from their teepee. Even today, Ihtsi-pai-tapi-yopa, the creator of all living things, was shining on them.

"All is in your hands," she whispered.

It wasn't long before Ni-namp'-skan was following her into Kitchi and Nuttah's teepee. His hair, twisted into a topknot, was gray, and his skin was lined from having seen many suns. But the old man had nimble limbs that Pi'tamaka had to take great strides to keep up with.

Swiftly he unrolled his tools from a tanned buffalo hide tied with a twig. Few words were exchanged as he swept his hands over Nuttah's damp forehead. With light hand motions he directed Pi'tamaka and Kitchi to get the fire blazing and to place two kettles with sarvis berries over it.

No one could make out the words he mumbled to himself as he swept around the teepee. Perhaps it was a prayer. Perhaps he was already talking with the spirits. Whatever the meaning, no one said anything for fear they might interrupt his work.

More sweeping hand motions directed them to bring large stones from the fire and place them around Nuttah. He draped several cow hides over her. From time to time Ni-namp-skan would sprinkle water over the rocks. Within hours, the little teepee that Kitchi and Nuttah shared turned into a steam lodge.

"The steam will draw out the illness." These were the only intelligible words Ni-namp'-skan said.

When not following the directions of Ni-namp-skan, Kitchi knelt by his wife's side.

"My love, you will get well soon." His encouraging whispers were repeated over and over again, humming like a chorus throughout the night. "It is but a cough, a headache, a light cold. Tomorrow is a bright new day and I will see you in good health."

But the feeling—like a pile of bricks leaning against Nuttah's chest—did not go away. Even with all of Ni-namp-skan's preparations and berries and prayers, the color did not return to her cheeks. Nuttah couldn't express this, but Ni-namp-skan knew it. Despite his tinctures and balms, it became clear to the old man. He had seen this too many times before.

"Tonight we must prepare to say good-bye." The wise man laid a heavy hand on Kitchi's shoulder. This is right. It is her time."

Before sunrise, the light in Nuttah's eyes that Kitchi adored so much faded. In the stillness of the night, Nuttah took her last breath.

Kitchi made a sound that few have heard before—a man whose heart has been clawed and beaten with the worst pain imaginable. It vibrated for miles and miles, across the rivers and mountains that surrounded his tribe, a stormy plea that shook the hearts of all who heard it.

"Poor Kitchi," the tribe's people said. "But, her time has come. Let us prepare for Nuttah's passing to the Sandhills."

Kitchi threw his body over his wife's. Her face became soaked with his tears as he buried his sorrow in her. "My love for you is more numerous than the stars in the night sky," he whispered. "It is more all-consuming and necessary than the buffalo."

Every memory he had of his wife suddenly flashed before his eyes— every spark of laughter, every night when their bodies slid together in wondrous love, every argument when her brows tilted, unsure of what the compromise would be. He brushed his tears off her sweet, moon-shaped face. Her lips still felt warm. Quickly, he got up.

"She's not dead," Kitchi said as he left his tent. Gently, he pulled shut the hide flaps that kept out the harsh winds. No one would enter.

"What did you say, Kitchi?" Pi'tamaka rose. In case she was needed throughout the night, she had slept on a mat outside of Kitchi and Nuttah's teepee.

"The air has barely left her body. Her soul hasn't moved on to the Sand Hills." He unwound the rope tied to a stick in the ground where his horse rested. Swinging his legs over his horse, he looked down at Pi'tamaka. "Be careful that no one touches my wife's body. I am going to the Sand Hills. I will find the one who has the spiritual magic to bring back souls to their bodies. And I will return with my wife!"

He leaned into his horse and sped off across the plains toward the rose-colored mountains.

He didn't carry water or dried meat to sustain him on his journey, thought Pi'tamaka. *He didn't even grab a spear in case he meets an enemy or needs to kill to survive. He's allowing himself to be driven by foolish emotion. But how long will he last out there?*

"Each of us is a vital thread in another person's tapestry. Our lives are woven together for a reason."[10] These were old words of wisdom Pi'tamaka had heard many times before. *Why was the puffy-faced boy who couldn't tie a rope properly brought into my life?* Pi'tamaka didn't know. But as a man, his broad shoulders had grown into a strength she could count on. *Rain, snow, or sunshine, he has always been by my side. Every person in our tribe is an integral part of our family. But perhaps since Father died, Kitchi has felt more important to me than all the others.*

Pi'tamaka unknowingly held her breath. No, that wasn't right. She merely felt saddened that her dear friend had lost his wife. She worried when she saw him ride off with no food or water. *That is it. That is how I feel.*

She wrapped hides around pieces of dried meat and berries and tied them shut with thin strands of twine. She filled two buffalo gourds with water and slung them over the sides of her horse. They would be heavy, but the journey through the plains toward the Sand Hills showed no promise of water. They'd need whatever provisions she could quickly wrap up and carry while riding out into the hot summer sun.

▲▼▲

By foot the journey from their camp to the Sand Hills would have taken four days. But on his horse, Kitchi knew he could reach the edge of the Hills when the moon was high in the sky, or at the latest, just before sunrise. His journey began with a wild show of strength and acceleration. Matching his own heightened emotions, his horse catapulted them onto the plain, throwing a stream of dust behind them. But after several hours, his trusty steed slowed her pace. Kitchi dismounted, giving them both time to rest. Staring at the short blades of grass offered nothing to Kitchi. It only made him anxious. With

---

10   Anonymous, n.d.

nothing to do but relive the night before with his wife, tears filled his eyes.

"Live your life for me," he thought he heard her whisper when his ear was close to her lips. But her breath was so strained, he hadn't been sure.

"Good-bye, Kitchi."

Horrified by the memory, he readied himself to mount his horse. *We must reach the Sand Hills by nightfall.*

A movement caught his attention—in the distance, a horse was riding from the direction of their camp. There was something about the rhythmic beat of the gallop that felt familiar to him. As each second drew the rider closer and closer to him, he felt a sense of calmness. When the rider came into view, he suddenly knew why.

"Pi'tamaka?"

The young huntress was startled to find Kitchi with his face soaked in tears. She quickly busied herself with untying her knapsack. She had been wise enough to pack food for them and their horses. Now, as the sun blazed over their heads, she could see that they greatly needed it.

"Drink," she responded, offering him a gourd. Turning toward his horse, she could see how deeply the animal heaved from tiredness.

"We will need to continue at a slower pace." Her voice was firm. She knew Kitchi might protest knowing that a slower pace would mean that they might not arrive at the Sand Hills until dawn. But if they didn't slow down, they might lose their horses. She placed her hand nurturingly over the panting animal. They had to take care of them.

"You don't have to come with me," Kitchi said.

Pi'tamaka turned to face him. It was the first time she had properly looked into his eyes since she stood in the doorway of his teepee the other day. All signs of the strength and joy she usually saw were gone. What stared back at her were chestnut-hued pools of grief hypnotized by pain. Why did it hurt her so much seeing her dear friend like that?

Life is not separate from death. It only looks that way.

This was another proverb she had heard throughout the years. It was what she wanted to say. But she knew that if she said it at this particular moment, she would regret it. It was too soon to begin dishing out proverbs. The best thing she could do right now was lead. It was what she did best. Instead of saying anything more, she carefully packed up their food and water. She mounted her horse and set a pace that would safely get the two of them to the Sand Hills.

That strange feeling of calmness came over Kitchi again as he mounted his horse and followed those beating braids. Hours later, he was surprised to look up and see that they were close to the rose-colored mountains. All day and all night they rode together silently at a steady trot across the plains. Pi'tamaka made them stop here and there so their horses could drink water. From time to time, she'd consult the constellations above them to ensure they were still traveling eastward toward the Sand Hills.

The journey should have felt hot, uncomfortable, and long. But somehow, with her in the lead, the hours felt like mere minutes to Kitchi. Now, under a starry sky and full moon, they were close to the Sand Hills. It was a short gallop to the rose-colored mountains, which had a garish tone to them in the moonlight.

Cradled in their shadows, Kitchi knew the Sandhills were there. Certain places could do this. The shadow at the base of the mountain drew his attention toward it. It felt almost hypnotizing. He couldn't look away. He could see nothing in the mist, and he wasn't quite sure if the whispers he heard were in his mind or came from the dark space itself. But he knew that whatever was there clawed at him and demanded his attention.

The comforting feeling rose again—Pi'tamaka wanted him to look in a different direction. Not too far from the path that led to the Sand Hills was a teepee. Smoke from the fire inside rose high in the night. His entire life he had heard proverbs about unity and the strength of togetherness. A tribe was the only way one could survive the harsh conditions of the plains. But here on a dark plain was a single teepee with no camp and nothing close to it for miles. Outside on a mat sat an old woman smoking a pipe.

Kitchi's legs ached as he dismounted. He wanted to continue riding to the Sand Hills. They were so close but still felt so far away.

"Why are you mourning?" The old woman said between puffs. She wore her hair long and loose, flowing behind her. It made her appear innocent and youthful, despite the many wrinkles that told her age.

"I am mourning for my wife." Kitchi found this to be an odd greeting, but he was eager to leave and go to the Sand Hills. She passed only last night. Now I am traveling to the Sand Hills looking for her," he replied.

The old woman said nothing in response. Instead, her eyes rested on Pi'tamaka. Kitchi could see that her silence and steady glare made Pi'tamaka uncomfortable. But the brave huntress didn't look away and kept a straight face under the watchful gaze.

"Is that so, young man?" at last she replied. "I have compassion for your pain and admiration for your bravery." Her gaze still rested on Pi'tamaka. "I will help you on this journey, but I warn you. Few who wander into the world of the dead ever return to the world of the living. Is your wife worth so much to you that you would sacrifice your life for this impossible quest?"

Kitchi pondered the woman's question. After much thought and an even stronger resolve, he answered, "My life is worth nothing without the woman I love. If there is but one teardrop's chance in a sea of tears, then I vow to give my all to this quest to bring my wife back to the land of the living. And if you would help, I'd be indebted to you and vow to repay you back as best I can in this life and the next."

At this the old woman looked at him. "Ah, young love! So fresh and exciting!" she laughed. "Certain things catch your eyes, but pursue only those that capture your heart." Her eyes quickly darted back to Pi'tamaka before turning toward Kitchi again. "But—there is no need for vows and payments. Young man, I help because I want to."

The old woman motioned for Pi'tamaka and Kitchi to follow her inside the teepee. Striped woven rugs were draped over the straw that was used to cover the earth, making seats around the fire. It burned gloriously, filling the space with bright light. As if she had been expecting them, Pi'tamaka noticed that there were three seats placed around the warm hearth.

"I know of Nuttah," the woman said as she tended to a cauldron that swung over the fire, dipping out stew into three gourds. "She, too, passed by this way only hours before you."

"What did she say? How did she look?"

Pi'tamaka cared for her friend, and seeing him so distraught secretly made her feel like she couldn't continue any further. It was the same feeling when he had ridden off across the wide plains without water for himself or his horse. Kitchi's emotions clawed at her own heart. The firelight flickered over his tears as he asked more questions about his wife and begged for the woman to help. But the old woman didn't have much to offer except words of wisdom and a warm meal to sustain them for the next part of their journey.

"Young man, I am a powerful woman. But this task is too powerful even for me. Still, I will do all I can to help you."

As the two hunters ate, the old woman rose to her feet and scurried around the lodge grabbing herbs—sweet pine, sage, and peppermint.

She wrapped them in a hide along with a buffalo stone. Pi'tamaka was surprised the old woman had one. She put it, along with the herbs, into a pouch she handed to Kitchi.

"These will help you." With a firm grasp her wrinkled hands clutched Kitchi's. "Now, you must listen carefully to the words that I say to you. Young man, this is a journey that will test your courage, heart, and loyalty. Only the dead can lead the living into the land of the dead. So I will go to the ghosts' camp to bring back someone to guide you. As you go on your journey, remember these three things.

"First, before you enter the camp, they will try to deter you and scare you away. *Do not be afraid, and stand strong in your task.*

"Second, they will hold a feast in your honor and try to entreat you to stay. Keep your heart pure. Eat only the herbs I have given you. Do not give in to the delicacies you see.

"Third, if you do make it this far, be warned that on your journey home you must close your eyes for the entire trip and listen only to the voice of your wife. Do not open your eyes until you are safe in the land of the living."

When her hands slipped away from Kitchi's, he felt a strange coldness. Intrigued by her words, he also felt her warning and softly repeated her instructions to himself. Despite the coldness in his fingertips, he noticed that the teepee was still warm when the old woman left and went out into the night.

Pi'tamaka tended to the fire. Much like the three seats that had been placed around the fire, Pi'tamaka noticed that there were three buffalo hides covered with wool blankets. Her brow furrowed. Two of them had been placed close together, while the third one was on the other side of the fire by itself.

As the embers of the fire quietly blazed, Pi'tamaka slid in between a mat and warm blanket. It felt good to finally rest her body after the long, emotional day. Kitchi slid onto the mat next to her. Turning to him, she felt like she had to end the day with something that could take away at least some of her friend's tears.

A proverb? Encouraging saying? A hug?

"It's nice to see that you'll achieve your wish," she said. But the words sounded clownish to her.

Did you not hear the old woman's warning? That was what she really wanted to say. *Let's turn back. Lest you lose your life, too, accept that all is as it should be. Even death is a part of life.* But she knew those words wouldn't make him feel any better. So instead of saying anything else, she fell asleep.

The cabin was dark when the woman entered again with a torch in her right hand.

"Wake up!" she whispered into Kitchi's ear. "As promised, I have brought a spirit of the dead to guide you through the Sand Hills. But you must hurry; they cannot be away for long. If the sun rises before they are back, their spirit will fade."

"Pi'tamaka?" Kitchi whispered in a sleepy haze.

The old woman grabbed Kitchi's hand before he could wake his friend out of her peaceful sleep.

"This is not her part of the journey."

Kitchi was disappointed he wouldn't have his friend by his side. But a part of him felt like he already knew she wouldn't be able to accompany him. Following the old woman, he left the warm hut for the cool night air.

"Kitchi!"

No one forgets the voice of their first love. The high little pitch she always made when she said his name—as though she were asking a question—it had only been two days—but Kitchi had feared he would never hear it again. He threw himself at the being standing in front of him.

"Is it you? Is it really you? How did you get here?" he exclaimed, touching every crevice of her face. "Never mind, let's go. We can leave this teepee and ride across the plain to be back home by sunrise."

Nuttah's soft laughter was just as he remembered.

"You'll have all the time you need to ask questions. But first I must return to the Sand Hills. And for this day—this day only—you'll come with me, my love."

Suddenly, something felt wrong. Kitchi roughly pulled away. She talked like Nuttah. She laughed like her too. But the scent of her hair was foreign to him. And her hand—the flesh was clammy and cold. In the moonlight there was a transparent tinge to her skin with outlines of fluorescent bones showing beneath.

Is she one of the spirits that the elders warned about—the ones who lured their relatives to their death?

"You sound like my wife," Kitchi stepped backward, staring into the brown eyes in front of him. No, it had to be her—the witty spark in her almond eyes was the same as he remembered.

"I am a spirit, my love," Nuttah said, looking down at her hands. "I am not a warm body like you remember. And I can't be. But—please accept me as I am so that we can talk. I will safely lead you to and from the Sand Hills, but if we do not go now, if the sunlight touches me, then even my spirit won't be able to stand before you."

With a nod from the old woman, Kitchi followed the spirit. She interlocked her fingers with his and the two walked toward the Sand Hills. Kitchi noticed that the dust their feet kicked up sparkled in the moonlight.

There wasn't a line of demarcation or some giant welcome sign that let them know they had arrived. But when they did, Kitchi felt it. The plains still stretched out before him. In the moonlight he could see smoke from camps of teepees in the distance. And the constellations and the mountains—none of that was out of the ordinary. But a feeling—a strange coldness that seemed to weave in and out around his body—welcomed Kitchi to the Sand Hills.

As cold as it was, the stars looked glorious that night.

"Do you love me?" Kitchi asked, ignoring the discomfort as he gazed at Aquila, Cygnus, and Lyra—the brightest stars of the sky—forming a triangle above their heads.

"Yes, my love." Nuttah's laughter was truly just as he remembered.

Even the light of the stars cannot match the beauty of your laugh.

"How much?" His teeth slightly chattered from the cold.

"I love you enough to defy the laws of our worlds and do the impossible. I love you enough to cross between worlds just to touch you." Nuttah playfully stroked his cheek, drawing an unexpected warmth into his body.

My beautiful wife, how you mesmerize me.

"My love," her tone became serious. "I must tell you something. Before the night is over…"

Suddenly, her words were interrupted. They had come toward a cluster of teepees, and Kitchi could hear bustling movements of men and women. But the signs of the Sand Hills were evident—like his wife's skin harshly translucent in the moonlight, so too was the camp around him. Everything had the soft haze of a dream. Even the sound of feet scuffling around him felt both far away and like a crazy pounding inside his head. Without warning, hundreds of spirits circled them with scorching shrieks that dropped Kitchi to his knees.

"Why are you here?"

"Go back to where you belong."

"Your scent—how vulgar. Leave at once!"

"You are not supposed to be here."

"Why are you here!"

The scathing remarks swarmed around Kitchi and Nuttah.

Do not be afraid, and stand strong in your task. Swiftly, he remembered the old woman's words. "I am here for my wife!" Kitchi's voice vibrated against the mountains.

The spirits were silent. Kitchi rose to his feet.

"I mourned her so much that, yes, I have come from the land of the living to the Sand Hills!"

A flutter of whispers spun around Kitchi.

"This is not good."

"He is not dead. He shouldn't be here."

"We have a chief. Let him decide this foolish one's fate."

The circle of spirits around the two lovers parted, creating a path that led toward a lodge.

Without hesitation, Nuttah grabbed Kitchi's hand to follow her as she stomped through the tunnel of spirits. Kitchi couldn't help but find comfort in seeing that familiar spark of her temper.

The lodge at the end of the path was unlike anything Kitchi had seen before. Where most stood at six or eight feet high, this lodge swept up into the sky at twice that height. Instead of sticks, the massive structure was held together by whole tree trunks. He was surprised to notice that unlike the other teepees he saw, this one didn't have a cold transparency to it. Inside, the splendor continued with an enormous fire burning with a ferocity that Kitchi had never seen before in the land of the living. Standing on the other side of this blaze sat the chief.

"My chief," Nuttah began. "I seek your kind ear and gracious judgment. For I have brought my husband from the land of the living for one night to be his wife. But the others condemn him. So I ask that you grant us this one night together."

Kitchi was startled to notice that a large black and white triangle had been painted across the chief's eyes and cheeks. It was the marking of a warrior, ceremoniously painted to ready him for war. A sea of feathers crowned the stern gaze that hardened at seeing Kitchi standing before him. Kitchi bowed his eyes in respect, remaining silent as his wife spoke.

"For love or not, it is a terrible thing that you have come here." The chief's voice felt like a flame leaping into Kitchi's ear. "You have disobeyed the laws of this world and that of the living."

The chief rose from his chair and walked around the fire to stand before Kitchi and Nuttah. Kitchi could see why the lodge was built so large. The chief was not an ordinary man. Had he been human, he would have stood at almost seven feet tall.

"It is more terrible that you have come and wish to leave. And it is very unlikely that you will ever leave, for no one from the land of the living ever has. But I will allow you one night."

Nuttah bowed before leaving the tent. Behind them, they heard the chief call out plans for festivities. A living man was walking through their camp, the chief said.

Instantly, his words brought raucous laughter and merriment. Instead of the terrifying slurs Kitchi had heard before entering the lodge, he walked out into a chorus of songs and playful jests as spirits offered him drinks. Outside, kids played games around a brewing bonfire while adults danced joyfully to the beat of flicking flames.

"The chief has granted you one night of safety here and, perhaps, safe passage. But do not for one minute forget the old woman's warning while you are here. Do not allow any food or drink to come to your lips." Nuttah slapped a drink out of Kitchi's hands, sending it rolling to the dusty earth. "I know that the old woman gave you herbs—sage and mint to cleanse and strengthen your spirit, and sweet pine for vitality. Eat only those."

The light of the bonfire lit up Nuttah's face. The wisdom in her almond-shaped eyes never ceased to astound Kitchi. None of this was what he expected. But he felt that whatever happened, they would be safe.

"Let's go somewhere quieter," she said as she looked at the revelry. "There are too many festivities here in the Sand Hills. Life is not as harsh here as it is on the plains of the living. Our food is ready. The winter doesn't come. And as you can see—look up—the stars are plentiful."

Amid the flashing crowds of spirits dancing and singing, Nuttah quietly cut through, holding Kitchi's hand tightly against her back. Leaving the bonfire far behind them, she led him out onto the dark plain, where it was so silent, Kitchi could hear his own heartbeat.

"Why are you here, my love?" she asked at last.

The question startled Kitchi. Does she not know? "I love you. And it's within my power to bring you back to the land of the living. I can't risk losing you forever. Especially when there's a chance that we can be together again."

"When we first met, I thought we would grow old together."

"But we had only three years."

Nuttah drew her lips tightly together, as if she was disappointed that he was counting the years. "Can't we say that we did grow old together during those three years?"

"But it isn't enough."

"But it could be."

"It still won't be—and we can do something about it," Kitchi protested.

"Do you think we would have had children?"

"We will have children. Keme and Kanti, named after our ancestors. A boy and girl," he said.

"Would she hunt like Pi'tamaka, or…"

Suddenly, the conversation frustrated Kitchi. What good were daydreams? They had one night to leave. Why were they not fleeing this place as she spoke?

"We'll still have children of our own, you know." He wondered if they'd have her wide almond eyes. "Everything we want will be ours. Nuttah, let's skip these dreams and make what we want real. I came here to find you. I have. Now why don't we go home?" He knew that she loved him, but he couldn't figure out why she was still standing there. *Why are we still here?*

"I'm a spirit now. So I'm not in only one place." There was a dreamy calmness to her voice that unsettled Kitchi. "I can see and hear even smell the incense burning in my father's home."

"I told them not to touch your body, to stay away so they wouldn't disturb you when you find your way back."

Nuttah shook her head. "I was sick, Kitchi. I thought you knew that. I cannot return to a sick body. It would be more painful and worse than death itself."

"But if you could be healed, then…" Kitchi's plea was lost in the silence of the night. His words were beginning to feel useless.

"Very true. One can be healed, but not after death. Even so, even with only three years, I'm content. Because I haven't left you." She took a deep breath before continuing. "Right now, I hear our fathers singing to me as they place my belongings around my body. I can almost taste the salty tears as Father tells me that we'll be together soon. He was the first to tell me that life is not separate from death—it only looks that way."

As Kitchi's eyes adjusted to the darkness—away from the light of the fires—he began to see more stars in the sky. There were so many of them. Some were brighter than others. But one cluster amongst the millions stood out to him the most. Most nights, or even years, he never saw Mensa, because the constellation contained no bright stars. But tonight, in the Sand Hills, the tips of his fingers clearly traced the stars of the cup-shaped constellation. In that outline of dimly lit stars, old words came to him.

"What is life? It is the flash of a firefly in the night. It is the breath of a buffalo in the wintertime. It is the little shadow that runs across the grass and loses itself in the sunset,"[11] Nuttah finished the proverb.

It was a saying that many elders had repeated since childhood. Nuttah's father had even woven it into his talk to them when they became family. Kitchi had always tried to listen to words of reason and wisdom. Now the words, flowing together with memories, comforted him.

"I'm not going to take you back home with me, am I?" It wasn't that he didn't know the answer. But somehow he needed to hear her say it.

---

11   Susan Ratcliffe, ed., *Oxford Essential Quotations*, 4th ed. (Oxford, UK: Oxford University Press, 2016).

"Many sunsets, I saw your wide smile as you rode home across the horizon. I know how much riding brings you joy. And I want you to know that every time you smile at the glorious plains stretched out in front of you, I'll be there in the shadows smiling back at you, Kitchi."

The emotions became too much. Every tear that Nuttah had held back since walking into the Sand Hills was released down her cheeks. But as Kitchi rushed to hold her in his arms, her tears quickly dried, and he was greeted with her wisdom.

"It's time for you to go back. The sun will be up soon."

"No, let me hold you a little longer," he said.

Without objection, Nuttah's arms clasped his neck. Just like all his memories, her cheek nuzzled into his broad shoulder.

Why can't this moment last forever?

"It's time. You must go back to the land of the living," she whispered.

A streak of lavender brushed the horizon. The sun would rise soon. As they walked back to the camp, Kitchi noticed that her grasp around his hand had strengthened.

"Stay with me, my love. Do not listen to them."

He wasn't sure what she meant at first. All the spirits were occupied with their drumming and songs and jumping dances as they drank and ate. But as Nuttah and Kitchi came closer to the land of the living, Kitchi noticed a change. At first it was just crooked smiles here and there turning toward him and eyes lingering too long on his face. But then he swatted away a light touch, then a grasp, and soon a multitude of hands grabbed at him. The journey through the camp became more difficult, and Kitchi saw the horizon growing brighter and brighter as the stars began to fade in the sky.

"When I was getting ready to meet you, Kitchi, I saw Pi'tamaka with you, just as I saw her ride out on the plains with you every morning." Somehow he could hear Nuttah's whispers above the crowd of spirits surrounding them. "I know she is your friend. But I can hear her heartbeat. And I can hear your name as she calls you. Don't be afraid to love again, Kitchi. We had three glorious years to grow old together. Mourn, but when it is time, open up your heart."

The weight of the spirits was becoming too much. Kitchi fought against it.

"Now listen to her voice. She's alive, and her voice will guide you back to the land of the living."

He fought against his wife's words. How could he lose her after he had come this far? But faintly, far in the distance somewhere, he thought he could hear Pi'tamaka calling his name. He turned toward Nuttah. *Is there still a chance that the two of us can make it back to the land of the living together?* But wherever he looked—his wife was nowhere to be found.

Do not open your eyes until you are safe in the land of the living. Again, the old woman's wisdom rang in his ears. At first, he wanted to protest, look around for Nuttah, but a tranquility suddenly swept over him. Calmly, Kitchi gave in and closed his eyes.

"Kitchi." The voice became louder. He knew for sure that it was Pi'tamaka. He couldn't see anything around him now, but he began to walk toward the sound. With each step the voice grew louder and louder and the weight from the spirits lifted. He felt like a man walking through a storm, one that was subsiding and allowing his foot to finally settle onto firm ground.

Eventually, the firm ground vibrated with the thuds of two feet rushing toward him. A shock of two warm arms cradled him, bringing a wave of new feelings that caused him to slightly blush.

"Open your eyes, silly. You're safe." Awash in tears, Pi'tamaka tried to pry his eyes wide open. "You're safe. You're safe." She continued her chorus of disbelief.

"When I woke up in the empty lodge of the old woman, I waited three days outside of the camp for you. I couldn't get in. I couldn't leave. All I could do was wait. It was only today that I thought to call your name. I was afraid that I had lost you."

Holding her tightly in silence, Kitchi understood everything. One night in the Sand Hills had been three in the land of the living. Nuttah knew that, just as she had known when it was his time to go back and when Pi'tamaka was calling him.

Was his wife right? Would his heart open up to feel love in that same way again? Right now, he wasn't sure. But while he held Pi'tamaka in his arms, he felt a familiar feeling of peace come over him. Right now he wanted to mourn with his dear friend.

He opened his eyes and stared out at the sunrise on the horizon. In the shadows of the rose-colored mountains, he saw someone familiar to him.

Do you love me? Kitchi whispered.

Yes, my love, I do.

Good-bye, they said to one another, knowing that it wouldn't be the last.

Nuttah's spirit faded, leaving the two friends alone, embracing one another on the plain.

"I can't believe it."

"You can't believe what?" Pi'tamaka said, drying her tears.

"There's very little difference between life and death," Kitchi said. "And I have experienced both. But now, let's go home."

FURTHER READING

The Homeric Hymn to Demeter by Homer

Devi Mahatmya, author unknown, but much like the Bible there are various translations

The Book of the Dead, author unknown, but much like the Bible there are various translations

Mythology of the Blackfoot Indians, compiled and translated by Clark Wissler and D. C. Duvall

ABOUT THE AUTHOR

Lindsay Christinee grew up in Pennsylvania enamored with historical biographies. To this day, she can still recite Nefertiti's full name (Neferneferuaten Nefertiti) or run through a list of England's queens. After she read about fashion greats Edith Head and Diana Vreeland, she parlayed her love of history into a fashion career in New York City showrooms. But it wasn't until moving to Bangkok that she began her writing career riding tuk-tuks as a ghostwriter for the city's English newspapers. In 2014, Lindsay moved back to the US, settling into Philadelphia's historic district and revitalizing her career to align with her environmental activism endeavors. Her words have been published in the Sierra Club, ReMake, *Reader's Digest*, and more, and she has spoken about sustainability and climate justice for podcasts and at schools in the Tri-State area. In 2020 she founded The Wellness Feed, a sustainable lifestyle website empowering its readers with conscious choices they can make to help mitigate climate change. *Myths of the Underworld* is her debut book.